Landing Your
First Job
Out of College

The Ultimate Job-Hunting Handbook

Landing Your First Job Out of College

Matt Gordon

St. Martin's Press   New York

Production Editor: David Stanford Burr

Library of Congress Cataloging-in-Publication Data

Gordon, Matt.
        Landing your first job out of college : the ultimate job-hunting handbook / Matt Gordon.
                p.   cm.
        "A Thomas Dunne book."
        ISBN 0-312-08813-2
        1. Job hunting.   I. Title.
    HF5382.7.G67   1993
    650.14—dc20   92-41750
                                                        CIP

First edition: March 1993

10 9 8 7 6 5 4 3 2 1

Contents

Acknowledgments

CAUTION: READING THIS PAGE WILL NOT HELP YOU LAND A JOB

First of all I would like to express my gratitude to my father and David Jones for their constructive criticism and thoughtful ideas. Next I would like to thank Julian Bach for his encouragement and wisdom. I would also like to thank Patty Rosati for championing my manuscript and guiding me through the publishing process.

Last, and most important, I would like to take this opportunity to thank my wonderful wife, Kathi, who suggested, encouraged and supported the writing of this book. As Ralph Kramden often said, "Baby, you're the greatest!"

Introduction

If you're looking for your first job, then this book was written for you. Whether you're certain about your career path, or have no idea what you want to do, this book will help you establish your criteria for your ideal first job. It doesn't matter whether you see yourself on a fast track to CEO, or just want a nine-to-five J-O-B: this book will teach you how to land the toughest job there is, your first. More important, it will show you how to get hired for the job you want, a crucial career-spanning skill that's often as important to a successful career as is doing a good job.

As you depart the ivory tower for the real world, it's time to utilize the most important concept you have learned in school: how to learn. As you read and use this book to conduct your job-hunting campaign, you should keep in mind your sole objective, which is to obtain one offer for the job you really want. Whether the economy is good or bad, unemployment is 2 percent or 12 percent, doesn't really matter. You're not looking to reduce unemployment from 10 percent to 5 percent. You're only looking to find one job that's right for you. It may feed your ego to get several offers and have a choice, but the reality is that you can only utilize one offer. Personally, I'd rather get only one offer, but have it satisfy all my key criteria.

Think of me as your own personal placement counselor. I'm going to coach you through every one of the seven basic steps required to land your first job and to get started on the right track for the career you want. Should you choose to utilize bits and pieces of this book, it will certainly improve your job-hunting skills. However, I would strongly encourage you to view this book as a process: one that will virtually guarantee your landing the first job that's right for you. Plan to read the entire book first and then use each chapter as a reference to aid you at each stage of your job search.

It's important to understand that getting your first job is not a race. Whether the job you want is waiting for you for five months before you graduate, or you land your ideal job six months after you graduate, you're a winner! You'll probably experience some frustrations throughout your job-hunting campaign. Almost everybody does. But if you stick with the program I've put together for you, you'll have a tremendous edge over your competition. You'll have the benefit of over eighteen years of my experience in corporate management, recruitment, and consulting to help make you a winner.

Landing Your
First Job
Out of College

Chapter One

"So, What Do You Want to Be Now That You're Grown Up?"

Establishing Your Criteria for Your First Job

Most people remember that classic scene in *The Graduate* in which Dustin Hoffman's proud parents throw him a graduation party. All their friends either ask him, "So, what are you going to do now?", or offer advice about what to do: *"Just one word: plastics."*

If you're like Dustin Hoffman was and don't know what you want to do with the rest of your life, or even what you want to do next, *Congratulations.* You are very normal. The truth is that you don't need to set an irreversible career track when you seek and accept your first job.

In fact, many successful people had first jobs in one field, and subsequent success in a totally different area. My favorite example is John Steinbeck, who was an apprentice painter, lab assistant, ranch hand, fruit picker, construction worker, and newspaper reporter before he started writing novels. Yet clearly, all of these jobs were building blocks in his foundation. Steinbeck went on and utilized what he had learned from each

1

"career." Could *The Grapes of Wrath* have been the book that it is without his firsthand experience?

Whether you know, or think that you know, exactly what you want to do, you should understand what a first job is, and there are only three elements: 1) experience, 2) building blocks, and 3) modest income.

Experience: I had a marketing professor in college who always told his students that "nothing worth learning can be taught; it must be experienced." People who've been to war and were in real battles rarely want to talk about it. If they do confide in you, the first thing they'll explain is that unless you've had the same kind of battlefield experience, there is no way you can really understand what it's like. The same concept holds true for working a full-time, career-path job. In my first six months as a brand assistant at H. J. Heinz, I learned at least ten times as much as I did in my entire MBA program.

Building Blocks: Whether you end up retiring from the first and only company you ever work for, or have the type of career that spans several companies and various industries or disciplines, you will want to: a) build a solid track record of accomplishments, and b) continually acquire new skills. In the last chapter of this book, I will give you a game plan to get your career started in the right direction.

Income: It should hardly ever be a consideration in your first job, if you are career driven. Even if Alex Keaton (Michael J. Fox on "Family Ties") is your role model and you religiously pray to the almighty dollar, *Don't focus myopically on starting salary!* First of all, with the exception of professional sports, starting jobs out of school will not make you rich immediately. Big compensation packages go to experienced, proven producers. Acquire the experience, skills, and track record first. Excellence in any field can be tremendously lucrative. The key is to be doing something you really love, so that you enjoy giving it a 100-percent effort. (Of course, it helps if what you love to do coincides with your strengths.) Forget about starting salary. The reality is that your standard of living will almost certainly be higher than it was in school. Besides, the big financial payoff (if that's what's important to you) is down the road a ways.

Let's say that you majored in accounting and are absolutely positive that you want to work for a Big Six accounting firm. You may even be certain that you want to specialize in corporate tax. Perhaps you have your BSME and, since you were ten years old, have always wanted to design jet fighter planes. Terrific, you are focused. You could almost skip the rest of this chapter, but I recommend strongly that you don't, for two reasons. First of all, after reading the rest of this chapter you may change your mind about what you want out of your first job. Second, if you don't change your mind, these exercises will only serve to strengthen your resolve. More important, they will help to crystallize *why* that's what you want, an essential selling point when you get to the job interview stage of the job-hunting process.

Two Not So Simple Questions

Before you start to put together your résumé, you should answer two questions. Before I get into the questions, I want you to understand that there are no a priori right and wrong answers. It is your life and only you can decide what's important to you. One person may believe that the only acceptable first job is an entry level field sales position with a blue-chip consumer products company, regardless of the initial territory (location). Someone else may believe that *anything* in Los Angeles that pays at least twenty-five thousand dollars per year is perfect. The only right answers are what's right for you. The only wrong answers come from not being honest with yourself. Once you've been working in the real world, your criteria may well change, and that's fine. Remember, you're not making a lifelong decision.

In my recruiting business, I regularly got calls from candidates along the lines of "Please get me out of metropolitan New

York," or "I cannot stand field sales anymore. How do I get into marketing?" Keep the proper perspective. Your first job is but a single step on a multidecade career path. You will always retain the right to change direction.

Where Do I Want to Live?

Probably the easier of the two questions. For some people there is only one city they will consider. For others, several cities may be equally appealing. Finally, there are people who are so focused on their early career path that obtaining the right entry level position in the right kind of company is their only goal, and location is irrelevant. Even if location is, at most, a tertiary consideration for you, I still want you to consider it as we establish your criteria. If nothing else, it may well serve as the tiebreaker if you're lucky enough to end up in the position of deciding between otherwise comparable offers in different locations.

Often the easy piece of the location puzzle is deciding where you wouldn't consider living. It may be the South, the Midwest, New York City, Los Angeles, or small towns. Take some time and think about it. No matter how important your job and your career are to you, you won't be working all of your waking hours. Where do you absolutely *not* want to be for your leisure time? Again, you are not making a lifelong decision. Your career may be so important to you that you're willing to live anywhere for a couple of years until you can acquire the track record and experience necessary to get both the job you want and the location you want.

If you don't ever want to shovel snow again, it's time to move south or west. If skiing is your passion, then the Northwest, Colorado, or New England could be ideal. If you can't live without an active single's social life, you'd better look near major cities. In short, until you retire (some thirty to fifty years from now), you're unlikely to have the flexibility that you currently have of deciding where you want to live. If you're following your fiancé(e) to graduate school or a job, then you've already decided on location, which has been mandated by other criteria that you deemed more important.

It's now time to establish the first of your criteria for your job search. List below, either in specific or general terms, locations that are either unacceptable or undesirable.

Totally unacceptable location(s), if any:

1) _____ Why? _____

2) _____ Why? _____

3) _____ Why? _____

4) _____ Why? _____

5) _____ Why? _____

Undesirable location(s), if any:

1) _____ Why? _____

2) _____ Why? _____

3) _____ Why? _____

4) _____ Why? _____

5) _____ Why? _____

Now that you've decided where you don't want to live, think about where you either insist on living, or at least would enjoy living.

Ideal location(s), if any:

1) _____ Why? _____

2) _____ Why? _____

3) _____ Why? _____

4) _____ Why? _____

5) _____ Why? _____

Desirable/acceptable location(s), if any:

1) _____ Why? _____

2) _____ Why? _____

3) _____ Why? _____

4) _____ Why? _____

5) _____ Why? _____

Location is only one factor to consider. It must be at least somewhat consistent with what you want to do. It's axiomatic that you won't find oceanographers living in Kansas City, or Fortune 500 CEOs in Fairbanks. Therefore, you're not finished finalizing the location issue until you answer the biggie:

What Do I Want to Do?

Properly answering "What do I want to do?" is the focal point of your first job-hunting campaign. If you don't know now, or are unable to decide between equally appealing alternatives, the following exercises will help you define the job(s) you want. Even if you know exactly what you want to do, you should complete this section in order to synthesize both *why* you want to, and what *skills* you offer an employer. Let's face it, both *why* you want to and what *skills* you offer are essential understandings for an employer to have about you before you will be offered a job. You certainly don't want to be in the position of refining your explanations to these questions while you're in the middle of a crucial interview for your ideal job!

What you're going to do now is to build the framework of your ideal job. Remember the ground rules. It's your life, and therefore, it's up to you alone to decide what you want. Just because Dad has his heart set on your coming into the family business, don't do it because he wants you to, or because it's easier than looking for a job you'd really like. In fact, if you really do want to enter the family business, you'll be much more valuable if you go to work for a competitor first for a couple of years. Then you will be able to bring some real-world experiences and some different approaches with you. And, they'll even pay you for the privilege. My advice is similar if your goal is to start your own business. Gain your experience and make your mistakes with someone else's money.

As you think about your first job, you have a plethora of issues to deal with. Large corporations offer training, exposure, and a "pedigree" for future job changes, but they are much more likely to be initially project-oriented. Smaller companies usually allow earlier hands-on experience, as well as greater exposure to the big picture, but less formal training. As you look down the road of your career path, keep in mind that it's relatively easy to go from a large corporation to a smaller business, but extremely difficult to leverage a good track record with a smaller company into a desirable middle management position in a large corporation.

Maybe your real goal is to start your own business in a couple of years and the breadth of experience you would gain at a smaller company is perfect for you. However, it's important to recognize that this decision could restrict your options should you change your mind.

Another consideration should be the culture of the organization. For example, large corporations are generally more structured and more political than smaller companies. Don't get hung up on the widely defined concept of "corporate politics." The real definition of corporate politics is simply dealing with people. Therefore, corporate politics will exist in any organization you join.

Some people are very concerned that everybody recognizes the name of the company they work for. When you say that you work at General Motors, IBM, or Nestlé, nobody responds, "Who?" to these household names. For seven years I worked for Norcliff Thayer, which would consistently elicit a puzzled response when I told people. Personally, it never bothered me, and I always enjoyed explaining that we were a division of Revlon and our businesses included Tums antacid and Oxy5/10 acne medication, names familiar to almost everyone.

Now it is time to decide what kind of a company you want to work for, and why:

My Ideal Company Profile

Company size: _____

Why?: _____

_____

Well known or not: _____

Why?: _____

_____

Privately or publicly held: _____

Why?: _____

_____

Well, now you know how you feel about being a big fish in a small pond or a small fish in a big lake, or if it even matters to you if you're in Lake Michigan or Wampus Pond. Your responses may be black and white, or you may be ambivalent about some criteria you are developing. Either way is fine. The key is to understand *why* you feel a certain way. Remember, when answering why in these exercises, that you'll never be able to sell a prospective employer until you've understood why and sold yourself.

"What do I want to do?" will probably be either the hardest or the easiest exercise for you in this chapter. If you majored in accounting, and want to be a CPA, what you want to do is pretty straightforward. However, perhaps you have more than one desirable first job; you would like to be either an advertising copywriter or a stockbroker. Let's assume that at this point, both appeal equally to you. If so, it means you should conduct a "simultaneous multicareer job-hunting campaign." As you go through the job-hunting process, you will undoubtedly learn more about each career path you are considering. When a preference emerges, I urge you to follow your newfound dream. Resist the temptation to accept an entry level job you are offered in what is no longer the field you really want.

If you think that you know what you want to do, and mutually exclusive first-job objectives are acceptable at this point, fill out your job objective(s) now. If you don't have that much direction yet, skip to the "five-year goals." You'll return to this exercise later.

As you fill in your job objective(s) below, put in the titles, functions, and even industries that describe as specifically as possible your personal Camelot. As you think about answering "why?", focus on two areas: what you do best (skills), and what your passion is.

My First Job Objective(s)

1) Ideal Job _____

_____

Why? _____

_____

2) Ideal Job _____

_____

Why? _____

_____

The "five-year goals" require you to think about where you would like to see yourself in five years. These should be goals that *currently* appeal to you.

My Five-Year Goals

Title _____ Income _____

Responsibilities/functions _____

_____

Personal (family, life-style, etc.) _____

_____

Compare your five-year goals with your Ideal Job. Are they consistent? Are they realistic? If not, you'd better rethink one or both of these areas.

Whether you have delayed filling out your ideal job or not, for now I want you to stop thinking about specific jobs, and focus introspectively. Who are you? What really excites you? What do you detest more than anything? Let's face it: We all give a better effort to something we love, and nobody gives their best effort to something they hate. A real job isn't anything like taking a course in school (three hours per week plus assignments). You'll be spending forty to sixty hours per week on your job. If you want to be successful, you had better really enjoy at least most of what you do.

Do you like working with people, or are you better with numbers and analysis? If you enjoy working with people, it could mean that sales, social work, or human resources is the best field for you. If you thrive on numbers and analysis, then you might think about market research or a Wall Street career. Are you happier being closely supervised in a highly structured environment, or would you prefer more freedom, such as a field sales job where you are trained, given a territory and minimal supervision, and rise or fall based on your quantifiable sales results?

Pretend that you're a young child sitting on Santa's knee, but instead of asking you what you want for Christmas, he asks: "What do you really like doing?" Fill in all five choices. If you have more than five, narrow your list down to the five most important.

What I Most Enjoy Doing

1) _____

   Why? _____

2) _____

   Why? _____

3) _____

   Why? _____

4) _____

   Why? _____

5) _____

   Why? _____

Finally, it's time to look at what you already bring to the party, that is, your applicable skills. Obviously you have, or will soon have, one or more degrees. You probably have some level of computer proficiency, or perhaps you have a fluency in one or more foreign languages. Maybe you played varsity sports and have developed a good style for being a team player, always an asset in the corporate world. You may be excellent with numbers, or write extremely well. Perhaps you have proven management skills from a summer job, or extracurricular activities such as being the editor of the school newspaper.

Take some time and think about your skills and strengths. List at least three and no more than nine skills and strengths that you believe you have. Put them in rank order starting with your number one best strength/skill:

My Skills and Strengths

1) _____

2) _____

3) _____

4) _____

5) _____

6) _____

7) _____

8) _____

9) _____

Don't worry if you currently lack all the skills necessary for the field you've chosen to enter. You'll get lots of on-the-job learning to fill in the gaps. If you had all the skills, you wouldn't be looking for an *entry level job.* However, be realistic. When I was growing up, I always wanted to be a singer and songwriter. My writing has always been good and creative. Unfortunately, I can't carry a tune. After a year of piano lessons, I thought I was making real progress when my piano instructor went to my parents and pleaded with them: "*Please,* do your son a favor, do me a favor, and stop wasting your money on piano lessons for him." Alas, I lacked the requisite skills, and my dream mercifully died.

If you've already filled out your Ideal Job exercise, you should review it for consistency with both what you like to do and your skills and strengths. If you want to be an accountant or financier, working with numbers should be high on your list. If what you like to do is inconsistent with your ideal job, then you'd better rethink your ideal job.

For those of you who have not yet filled out your Ideal Job exercise, look at your "What I Most Enjoy Doing" list and your skills/strengths list and your five-year goals. As you compare them, look for a picture to emerge. (Some people find it helpful to make a similar list of the five things that they least enjoy, and why.) If, after performing this self-evaluative multiregression analysis, you do not discover one or more first jobs that would appeal to you, go to your placement office and share your lists and your thinking with a counselor and ask for help.

At this point you should have a clear idea about what you're looking for, as well as what's important to you. You should be able to verbalize in one or two sentences what you're looking for in your first job. Your description should include both your *essential* criteria and your *desirable* criteria.

Here's a personal example of my clearly defined objective for my first job: "I'm looking for an entry level opportunity in brand management (classic consumer products marketing) with a blue-chip company. Ideally, I would like to be able to live in New York City."

There it is in only two sentences. The first sentence was my "essential criteria." The second sentence was my "desired criterion." I got my MBA in 1973, then spent a year in VISTA (Domestic Peace Corps). I started looking for my first job in September of 1974, in the middle of a recession, when companies were either reducing or eliminating entry level training programs, just as they have in the early 1990s. I had known for over ten years what I wanted to do, and this two-sentence statement was my personal resolution. It is a matter of fact that I turned down two jobs in New York City—one offering one third more than my eventual starting salary—because they failed to meet my essential criteria. My "essential criteria" were fulfilled in November, when H. J. Heinz in Pittsburgh offered me a job as the brand assistant on Heinz Chili Sauce and Heinz Barbecue Sauce. I sacrificed my desired criterion (living in New York City) to fulfill my essential criteria. I got what I really wanted, but only because I did the exercises in this chapter and *knew* what I really wanted.

The *final exam* for this chapter is pass/fail, and you do the grading. Write down your objective statement(s). It/they should include your essential criteria and your desired criteria. It should be no more than four sentences. The more concise you are able to make your statement, the better. Now, starting with your essential criteria, write down your statement for each Ideal Job you are pursuing:

My First Job Objective Statement(s)

1) _____

_____

_____

_____

2) _____

_____

_____

_____

3) _____

_____

_____

_____

Now that you know what you want, you too can get the kind of job that you really want.

Chapter Two

All About Résumés

How to Look Better "On Paper" than Your Competition

Résumés are often fragile documents. Once they have developed a résumé, most people are overly resistant to changing any part. Yet, almost everybody has a different idea about what constitutes an excellent résumé. Show one to six executive recruiters and you will receive at least seven different approaches to making it better. As you gain full-time experience, it will change, both in format and substance. Your single-minded focus should be on creating a résumé that will maximize the number of interviews you get for your first job out of school.

Most college placement offices now have computerized formats for résumés. You will probably need to use them for on-campus interviews arranged through your placement office. However, I've yet to see one that I'd want to use. You still need a great résumé, even to supplement the placement office form.

Before I get into the mechanics of putting together your résumé, I'd like to clarify both why you need one and what it can and cannot do for you. First of all, the business world is conditioned, like a Pavlovian dog, to shake hands and say: "It's nice to meet you. May I see your résumé please?" While it's highly unlikely you will even obtain a job interview until they've reviewed your résumé, not having one for a face-to-face interview will distinguish you from your competition in a way that you don't want. Conversely, having a well thought out, properly presented résumé will establish you as a cut above the other applicants and favorably predispose the interviewer toward you.

Résumés are one of the key tools you must have in your job-hunting campaign toolbox to get that first job. However, they are only one of the necessary tools. *Nobody was ever offered a job from a résumé alone!* They can help you get interviews; they can even set a favorable tone and provide a framework for a successful face-to-face interview. But that's their total utility. Period.

Since we've established the necessity of having a résumé, and noted that it is a key to unlocking interviewing opportunities, why not have the best one possible? It will cost you the same dollars to print and utilize a lousy résumé that it will cost you to print an excellent one. Believe me, excellent résumés stand out.

As an executive recruiter, I saw thousands of résumés a year. I would rate less than 5 percent as very good or excellent. I don't think I will ever cease to be amazed at the frequency of badly written résumés I see from executives making $50,000 to $150,000 per year. These executives can grow sophisticated businesses by tens of millions of dollars, but fail to approach "selling themselves" with the same discipline, sophistication, and commitment they use to run their businesses.

Your single-minded objective with your résumé is to make it so persuasive that you get an opportunity to sell yourself in a face-to-face interview. It must stand out from the dozens (even hundreds) of others that represent your competition. I'm often asked if it's what you say or how you say it that matters the most. The answer is that they're both equally important. You will need to utilize the same skills used by copywriters, art directors, and strategic planners.

In a meeting with recent college graduates still looking for their first job, several told me that their well-meaning parents were paying a "pro" to write their résumé for them. Please don't make this mistake! Your résumé is a "selling sheet" for a unique product, and *you* are the product. Nobody knows that product 10 percent as well as you do—certainly not a stranger. A basic key to successful selling is knowledge, and you are the most knowledgeable expert on yourself.

In this chapter I will cover everything you need to know to put together a topflight résumé. First, I'm going to discuss what *not* to put on it. Then, together, we'll work step by step to create a truly superior document.

Almost every résumé that I see, even from directors and vice-presidents, contains one or more pieces of information that belong in what I call Never Never Land, as in they should never, *never* land on a résumé. One of the most common mistakes is to include "self-evaluative" phrases, words like "bright, quick study" or "energetic." They should be avoided at all costs. From a potential employer's standpoint, it's presumptuous, at the very least. These personal attributes should be saved for demonstration during the face-to-face interview, where the hiring decision will be made.

Your résumé should be a factual biographical picture, with the sole objective of *screening you in* for the face-to-face interview. If you put too much on it, it's more likely to screen you *out.* By the way, while I used the metaphor of "painting a picture," unless you want to be a model or an actor, never include a picture of yourself.

Another one-line space waster is "References available on request." Everyone will need references before he or she is offered a job, and it's assumed that you can furnish them. Don't waste the precious space and clutter your résumé.

Related by blood to "References available" is the unusual and revealing "Health excellent." Maybe it would be relevant if you were applying to Outward Bound. I've never seen a résumé with "Health fair" on it. Again, save that valuable space for something significant.

Another space waster is heading your résumé with the word

Résumé, or even worse, *Confidential Résumé.* All résumés are confidential.

Salary objectives also belong in Never Never Land. Aside from wasting space, they can only accomplish two things for you, and both of them are bad. First of all, salary objective statements can result in your not being considered for a job you'd want, and otherwise might get, because your objective is either too high or too low. Second, it might result in your being offered a lower starting salary than the employer intended, because your objective is less than the employer was expecting to pay.

The final area in Never Never Land is "Geographical Preference." Even if you have strong preferences or severe restrictions, all it can do is screen out opportunities you might otherwise make an exception for. Employers are looking for entry level people who are open, willing, and able. Restricting geography undermines your commitment. Maybe the job they're considering you for fits your short-term geographic needs but will require a relocation in a year or two, and that's not a problem for you. But, after reading your geographical preference, they decide to interview other candidates who don't have such potential restrictions. In short, you can target the geography that appeals to you by whom you approach, where you interview, and ultimately by where you accept a job. The idea is to maximize your options by at least appearing to be flexible.

Now that we've exiled all those space wasters to Never Never Land, it's time to put together an excellent résumé, with the single-minded objective being to maximize the number of face-to-face interviews you will generate. I'm going to guide you line by line, but first, I need to make some overview comments.

Think of your résumé as a vehicle to create an overall, factual picture of yourself. Though it only loosely defines who you are, it does historically describe what you've done, and forecasts your ability to contribute.

Remember, *brevity* is the only acceptable style for the corporate world. When three words accurately describe something, don't embellish. Let your résumé foreshadow your ability to communicate in the style of the corporate world, that is, accurately and as briefly as possible.

We've already eliminated the unnecessary and harmful space wasters that clutter a résumé and divert attention from the key selling points. But it's the proper use of *white space* that improves readability. Ask any advertising pro or look at successful print ads and you'll note that it's the white space that makes them pleasing to the eye and easy to read. Therefore, your margins should be at least one inch, and this applies to all four margins: top, bottom, right, and left.

The next rule that you must follow is to create your résumé on *one page* (8½″ × 11″). Until you have at least three years of experience, your résumé should be *one* page. Even if you have worked somewhere for a year or two and then gone back to school, keep it to one page. Please, don't even think about a bigger page like 11″ × 17″, or printing on both sides of a page. How can you expect to be asked to join an organization if you initially approach them by breaking the unwritten rules?

Finally, your résumé must score 100 percent on both *neatness and accuracy*. There must not be a single typo! Have at least two friends proofread it *before* you have it printed. If you have access to a word processor, neatness, layout, and spelling accuracy should be easy to achieve.

Unless your objective is a career in a highly creative field like design, advertising art, etc., use plain white or off-white paper. Also be sure to use good quality paper and offset printing. If you have access to a good quality laser printer, fine. Generally, you'll find that offset printing will be the most cost efficient.

I would suggest printing at least two hundred copies for each Ideal Job you intend to pursue. You might be able to get by with one hundred, but you won't save very much money, and it will cost you much more in total to print an additional one hundred than it would have if you had originally ordered two hundred. Remember, your objective is to get the right job. Would you honestly be upset if you had one hundred and twenty copies left over after landing your Ideal Job? It's more important to always have a copy of your résumé available, so think of it as insurance. It's difficult enough having to find your first job out of school.

Don't miss out on a great opportunity because you're temporarily out of stock on résumés.

The next few pages show you three excellent résumé models. Now honestly, wouldn't you want to interview Gail for an entry level position in sales? Wouldn't you like your résumé (on page 22) to be just as impressive? It can be.

Look at two more résumés (pages 23 and 24) before we start to put together your résumé. Notice on Robert Jones's résumé under experience that the job titles are listed before the company. The reason for this is that given Robert's job objective, his titles are more impressive than the places he worked.

Don't both Robert and John, like Gail, appear to be interesting, talented people who are loaded with potential? It's time to make your résumé equally impressive. Get out a pad of paper and a pen or pencil and let's begin.

1 ▪ *Name:* Use all capital letters if you prefer, but definitely use the same size type as the rest of your résumé. Flaunting your ego with extra large type for your name not only wastes valuable space, but it looks bad. Don't use titles like Mr., Ms., or Mrs. Middle name and/or initial(s) are optional. If you go by a different name from your given name (such as Bob or Bobby for Robert), use whatever you're most comfortable with. My personal preference is to use the name your friends call you, or what you'd like them to call you.

If you have a stuffy name, you should soften it, if possible. You'll find that a lot of people in the corporate world came up from the school of hard knocks. Taking the résumé of Gustav Heinrich Von Mueller IV and sending it to the "round file" gives them a moment of true pleasure. Gus Von Mueller, on the other hand, could be just what they're looking for. You can either center your name—my preference—or skew it to the left, whichever you think looks best.

2 ▪ *Address(es) and Phone Number(s):* This *crucial* contact information should be right below your name, where it's

Gail Barker
27 Elm Street #10A
Champaign, IL 61820
217-335-5253

OBJECTIVE: Entry level opportunity in sales

EDUCATION: University of Illinois—B.A. May 1993
Major: Art History   GPA: 3.2/4.0

Activities:
Business Manager, *Daily Illini* Newspaper
(increased ad revenues +23%)
Illini Debating Team
Rush Chairperson, Delta Delta Delta Sorority

Self-financed 75% of education

EXPERIENCE:
Summers of   *Good Humor Truck Route Salesperson*
1990–1992

· Averaged +32% sales increase vs. prior year
· Ranked #1 in region in 1992
· Ranked #2 nationally in 1992 and #7 in 1991

Summer of   *Tour Guide—Chicago Museum of Modern Art*
1989

· Received "Summer Intern of 1989" Award

PERSONAL: Single
5'5", 115 lbs.
Hobbies: chess, tennis, camping, and reading
Computer literate (Lotus)
Fluent in Spanish

Robert Jones
170 Frankie Way
New Haven, CT 06513
203-248-1569

OBJECTIVE: Entry level management position in communications

EDUCATION:

Fairfield University	Fairfield, CT
Bachelor of Arts	May 1993
Major: English	GPA in major: 3.75
Minor: Philosophy	GPA overall: 3.44

Dean's List—five consecutive semesters

Course Highlights: Contemporary Journalism, Corporate Communications, Media and Society, Speech Writing and Delivery, Freelance Journalism. Proficiency on Apple Macintosh and WordPerfect 5.0.

ACTIVITIES:

President, English Club
Assistant Director, Transfer Orientation
Vice-President, English Honor Society
Student Advisor

EXPERIENCE:

Intern: *Dental News* Sept. 1992–Apr. 1993
Edited and proofread material for publication. Wrote uncredited material and product news. Provided input on editorial focus. Systematized subscription files. Perfected word processing skills.

Writing Center Tutor Sept. 1992–May 1993
Selected to be member of pilot group. Listened, clarified, questioned, and responded to undergraduate students' writing concerns during private tutoring sessions.

Assistant Editor: *The Forum* Spring 1992
Reviewed and selected manuscripts for publication. Worked with writers in editing their material. Assisted Editor with layout and production.

Host: Evelyn's Restaurant Summer 1992
Trained new employees, assisted in planning large parties, and developed new customer relations policy.

PERSONAL:

Single, born 4/10/71
Hobbies: Reading, bridge, bicycle touring

John Newman
28900 Cortez Ave. #7
San Jose, CA 94016
408-974-9634

OBJECTIVE: Entry level opportunity in marine biology research

EDUCATION: San Jose State   B.S.   May 1993   GPA 3.2/4.0
Major: Marine Biology   Minor: Asian Studies

Brosco Award (original research in marine biology)
nineteen ninety-two
Vice President ATO. Coauthored: "The Effect of Acid
Rain on Freshwater Shrimp Larvae," presented to the
Marine Biology Research Association 10/14/92 at
annual convention

EXPERIENCE:
5/92–9/92   *Larkspur Preserve*   Carson City, NV
Worked summer job in hatchery and fishing
preserve. Exposure and duties ran the spectrum
from breeding and feeding to sorting. Diagnosed
rare bacterial enzyme culture which had been
causing stunted growth in male brown trout.
Suggested midweek day fishing promotion which
increased revenue +36% during slow Monday
through Thursday period.

summers of   *Mazola Builders*   San Jose, CA
1989–1991   Worked three summers for independent home
builder to help finance education. Having worked on
all phases of home construction, offered
apprenticeship upon graduation.

1988–1993   Various part-time jobs in Student Union Dining Room
(dishwasher, busboy, waiter) to help finance education.

PERSONAL: Single, born 5/1/71
Hobbies: scuba diving, fishing, oil painting

easy to find. Ideally you should have an answering machine. Business people are conditioned to expect to be able to leave a message if you're not there. If you don't have one, and cannot afford an answering machine/answering service, you *must* have an alternate phone number (such as your parents) where a message can be left for you. Who knows how many opportunities are missed because after calling you two or three times and getting no answer, a busy executive decides to try another candidate who looked just as promising? Nobody looks so attractive on paper, for an entry level job, that a company will go to extraordinary lengths to contact them for an interview.

3 ▪ *Objective:* Remember the exercises you completed in Chapter One, culminating in a concise statement of your objective(s). This is where you start to put it to work for you. Every word must be carefully chosen. Only include your essential criteria for your objective. You can always reject an offer or an opportunity that's not right for you, but the opportunity that you might have loved but never heard about, because your objective statement screened you out, is a lost opportunity, forever.

If your objective is to simultaneously pursue more than one field, *do not use a conjunctive objective statement.* It lacks the conviction employers seek in entry level candidates. Therefore, you'll need a unique objective statement for each separate area in which you have an interest. Generally, the remainder of your résumé will be identical.

Remember my personal first-job objective statement at the end of Chapter One: "I'm looking for an entry level opportunity in brand management (classic consumer products) with a blue-chip company. Ideally, I would like to live in New York City." When I translated that to my objective, it read: *Objective: entry level opportunity in brand management.* The rest of my statement could only serve to screen out opportunities that I might have considered.

4 ▪ *Education:* The résumé that you put together for your *next* job will be organized with "Education" following

your "Work Experience" section. However, résumés should be in a reverse chronological format, and your most recent accomplishment is the degree you are soon to receive or have just received. Even if you have full-time, relevant work experience, your most recent accomplishment, your degree, should come first. You would make an exception to this rule if you had been working full-time and going to school at night. However, then you're no longer in the position of getting your first job. If you have more than one degree, list them in reverse chronological order (that is, most recent to least recent).

List the school first, followed by the degree and the date received. Personally, I prefer using both the month and the year(s) for dates. It demonstrates both honesty and attention to detail. The next line should include your major(s), and if relevant to your objective, your minor(s).

Grades are a touchy subject, unless they're very good. Basically, you have three options. You can put down your actual grade point average. You can put down your grade point average in your major (properly labeled) if it's significantly higher. Finally, you can ignore your grades altogether on your résumé. Even if your grades are excellent, if your résumé is too long, you can omit your grades. Employers who really care about grades will ask about them. Think how impressive it would be to say, "I have a 3.7/4.0," and to have omitted that from your résumé. You also have the option of putting your grades down without clarification, for example, 3.1 GPA instead of 3.1/5.0. Personally, I think you're better off to omit your grades than mislead in any way.

My own belief is that grades in school are not a reliable predictor of success in the business world. Years ago I attended graduation ceremonies at a prestigious school and the commencement speaker made a statement to this effect: "In particular today, we are here to honor the *A* and *B* students, as well we should. Many of them will go on to teach at this and other hallowed institutions of higher learning. But, we should all pay homage to the *C* and *D* students as well, for history has taught us that they are the ones most likely to donate the money for the buildings that the professors will teach in."

My personal bias aside, some employers will have rigid guidelines about acceptable grade point averages. Most will at least ask about grades, especially if you don't put them on your résumé. I do know of cases in which a candidate omitted grades from the résumé, and got so far along in the interview process and was able to impress enough people that even a major accounting firm made an exception on their minimum acceptable GPA and made him an offer.

My advice is, if you have good grades, flaunt them. Otherwise, do what you feel comfortable with. If you're struggling with this issue now, trust me: two years from now nobody will care what your grades were, including you. The issue will be: What have you accomplished since you started working?

The next section under "Education" will include academic honors, awards, and extracurricular activities. Start with the most impressive. If the list is too long, a nice problem, you should omit the least relevant and least impressive. You want to look like a focused winner with significant accomplishments, not a dabbler or a dilettante.

Finally, if you financed *any* part of your educational expenses (including living expenses), through scholarships, working, or whatever, make certain to use this very impressive phrase: "self-financed × percent of education."

If you have more than one degree, repeat this process for each degree that you have.

5 ▪ *Work Experience:* Again, reverse chronological order starting with your most recent job. If you have had lots of menial part-time jobs in which all you got was a paycheck, by all means lump them together. You've already credited yourself with them under *"self-financed × percent of education."*

To the extent possible, after listing each meaningful job,

with dates including months, *focus on one or two tangible accomplishments,* and whenever possible, *quantify* them. At the very least, crystallize something relevant that you learned from the experience. Companies want to hire people who will make contributions. If you've made contributions in past jobs, it's logical that you'll do the same for them. The best contributions are either increased sales and/or profits or reduced costs, including time-saving ideas which reduced costs and therefore increased profits. No matter what you decide to put down, *your objective must be to demonstrate that you: a) have contributed, and b) have learned from the experience.* But don't ever fake anything. These are the areas that savvy employers will probe in the interviewing process, and if you don't seem to understand what you have put on your résumé, they will see this immediately. On the other hand, if a potential employer sees that you were able to learn and make meaningful contributions at a summer or part-time job, imagine how much you could contribute on a full-time basis.

6 ▪ *Skills:* This section is optional, depending on what, if any, specific skills you bring to your new employer. If you're fluent in a foreign language, by all means, put it down. It's always impressive, even if you're not looking for an international assignment. If you have any level of computer proficiency, put it here. If you've picked up any relevant certifications, put them here. However, the certification must project into a potential benefit for your prospective employer. Being a certified Red Cross lifeguard won't excite most companies to save a slot for you.

7 ▪ *Personal:* Your first résumé, right out of school, is the one and only time it is acceptable to include hobbies and interests. Interviewers will often pick up on something from this section to put you at ease for the interview. However, select with care and think about the implications. Hobbies such as chess and bridge require logic,

strategic thinking, and analytical ability. Maybe you even have a national ranking or certification to brag about! Don't be shy about your accomplishments when you're putting your best foot forward.

Something like "watching sports on TV" may be how you spend most of your free time, but it certainly doesn't convey the "doer" image that mountain climbing and playing tennis do. Any articles or books that you have had published are definitely worth listing. While unusual hobbies make for interesting conversation at cocktail parties, hobbies and interests tied to accomplishments make for interesting candidates.

Finally, consider concluding the personal section, and your résumé, with your vital statistics: date of birth and marital status. While height and weight are optional, I would counsel you to include them. It completes the picture of being open and honest with nothing to hide—someone who knows who he/she is, and has self-confidence. After all, they're going to meet you in person anyway. Isn't it better to warn them if you're a midget, obese, "physically challenged," etc.?

Once you've fine-tuned your résumé, put it away for a few days, and finish reading this book. Then, go back over it to see if it shouts: *Ready, Willing, and Able!* Double-check to make certain that you haven't violated any of the sins of Never Never Land (see boxes on page 30).

Be sure to show your résumé to your friends, placement counselor, and any executives you may know. Listen to their comments and think about them objectively. If *you* believe their idea(s) will improve your résumé, then incorporate them and improve it. If you have followed the guidelines that I've given you, there's no reason that your résumé can't be in the top 5 percent of your competition.

As we wrap up this section, I'd like to leave you with an anecdote that reinforces the adage that "honesty is the best policy," not only on résumés, but for the entire job-hunting process. Several years ago a friend of mine was about to hire a recent college graduate for a job as a Wall Street trader. That night at dinner he told his son that he was going to hire one of the section directors from the camp he had attended the last three summers. His son asked which section, and when told replied in astonishment, "You're going to hire Barry!" Upon further checking my friend discovered that his candidate had been a "senior counselor," not a "section director." He immediately rescinded his offer. The irony is that he would have been hired had he been honest about his relatively meaningless summer job. As my friend confided in me, "How can I hire someone to become a trader if I can't trust him?" Need I say any more about honesty?

Never Never Land Checklist

1 ▪ Self-evaluative phrases

2 ▪ "References available," "Health excellent," and "Confidential Résumé"

3 ▪ "Geographical Preference"

4 ▪ "Salary Objective"

5 ▪ Wordiness

6 ▪ Photo

Successful Résumé Checklist

1 ▪ **Layout**—good margins, no typos

2 ▪ **Objective** Statement—clear and terse

3 ▪ **Education**—focused relative to job objective

4 ▪ **Experience**—focused first against job objective (if possible) and second against self-financing education

Chapter Three

Generating Interviews

Ideas, Strategies, and Guerrilla Warfare Tactics

John Wanamaker once said something to the effect that he knew he was wasting half of the money he spent on advertising. The problem was, he never knew which half was wasted, so he maintained his entire advertising budget, because overall, it was effective. The exact same principle applies to generating job interviews. Most of your efforts will be wasted, but you will not know up front which ones. However, the more efforts you make, the more interviews you'll generate. It's axiomatic that the more interviews you can generate, the more likely you are to get the job you want.

"Thanks, but no thanks" letters, or rejection by any other means will predictably be the results of most of your efforts. I'm not trying to discourage you; in fact, quite the contrary. If you're managing your job-hunting campaign correctly, every rejection is actually a step closer to your objective. It's important to continually remind yourself that your *sole* objective is to get *one good offer,* that is, an offer that meets your essential criteria.

It doesn't matter how many rejections you get, or even how many offers you get, as long as you get one right offer. However, before you can expect any offer, you'll need to generate interviews.

Developing Your Hit List

School Placement Office: The first place to start is your school placement office. Get registered and familiarize yourself with both their process and their resources. Find out about all the resources they offer, and take advantage of them. Thousands of companies go to many college campuses regularly to hire for entry level jobs for people right out of school. However, there are a few reasons why you should not rely entirely on the placement office to generate all of your interviews. First of all, the companies or industries that interest you may or may not be coming to your school to interview. Second, you're likely to be limited in how many companies you can interview with through the placement office. (That's why you must learn and understand their process early, so you can maximize the benefit to you.) Finally, campus interviews are short, usually about thirty minutes, with each company recruiter seeing upwards of twenty candidates per day. No matter how good you are, you need be very lucky to stand out in the recruiter's mind, and be asked back for a full day of interviewing at the company.

Please don't misunderstand. Take full advantage of as many on-campus interviewing opportunities as possible; just don't rely on them exclusively. There are many reasons why every year only 30 to 55 percent of college graduates have jobs waiting for them when they graduate. Assuming that everybody gets their first job through their school placement office—and they don't—the placement office alone is no better than a fifty-fifty proposition.

Make certain that you get the full list of which companies are coming to your campus. Consider trading lists with your friends at other schools, where different companies may be recruiting. Any companies that interest you, but are unable to accommodate you for an on-campus interview, should be put on your "hit list" of target companies. I will tell you later in this chapter the most efficient way to approach these companies, but for now, you need to develop a list of companies that you think you'd like to work for. Companies that interview on your campus will represent only a small fraction of the opportunities that would satisfy your first-job objectives. Yes, developing your "hit list" is going to be a lot of work, so the sooner you get started, the better off you'll be. If you're able to nail down the job you want before you graduate, terrific. You'll be able to relax and really enjoy the remainder of your school career.

If you've already graduated and still don't have a job, relax; you're in the majority, and this chapter is exactly what you need to jump-start your job-hunting campaign. Sure, you need to get busy, but employers respect candidates who wouldn't settle for a job that wasn't what they really wanted. Maybe you'll luck out and find an entry level job that someone else accepted, but then turned down at the last minute. At the very least, you're in a position to devote 100 percent of your time to finding the job you want.

There's also a silver lining to having trouble finding your first job. You'll really learn a very important skill—how to find and interview for a job. As your career advances and you look to leverage your career by changing companies, you'll be light years ahead of the class valedictorian who got a job right out of school in just a couple of interviews. That poor person hasn't learned anything about job hunting or interviewing.

The Library: The library is another good source of employment information. If you're focused on one or more industries, read through the applicable industry publications. If geographical considerations are important to you, look at the Sunday help wanted ads in those local newspapers. Scour the business telephone directory for companies in your targeted geography. In addition, most states publish a state manufacturing directory, broken out by industry codes (known as SIC, or Standard Industrial Classification).

If your interest lies in a particular industry, there's probably an industry directory that lists names, addresses, and the companies you'd be interesting in pursuing. Find out either where the industry association or the industry tabloid is located. Call or write to obtain an industry association list with contacts.

The list of appropriate reference books available is extensive. I have included many of them in the *Appendix* for your hit list. Find the ones that serve your needs and utilize them.

I'm often asked, "How many companies should be on my hit list?" I always have the same answer: "It depends on how badly and how quickly you want to find the right job." For every hundred companies you approach, you'll do well to generate five to ten interviews. If it takes you ten interviews to learn the "interviewing game" (see Chapters Four and Five), then you'd better have at least two hundred companies on your list. If you want to overcome bad luck, bad timing, and offers that don't really meet your essential criteria, I'd suggest that you approach at least three hundred companies, or more.

After you do your research, you should have a targeted hit list of hundreds of companies with address, phone number, and a specific person to contact. It's always best to have a person's name. Corporate junk mail is immediately identified by an address that includes a title only, without a name. The ideal contact is the department head of the function that you're interested in. If you're looking for an entry level job in corporate finance, write to the divisional controller. You can always send your letter and résumé to Human Resources, but if the department head forwards your correspondence, it carries added clout. In addition, you've initiated contact with someone who probably started out in the same kind of entry level job you're seeking. If there's nothing available for you there, the department head is in a position to give you some helpful advice, ideas, and perhaps a referral.

Answering Ads: You won't find many ads for entry level jobs, but when you do, you should answer them if they're on target with your objectives. A worthwhile gambit is to answer ads for candidates with "1–3 years experience." Write them and say, If you'd hired someone like me a year ago, you wouldn't need to be looking outside to fill this job. While it won't happen often, I've seen people create an entry level job in a company that doesn't usually hire people without experience.

Alumni: Go through the last two to three years of your school's alumni magazine and look through the class notes section. Find alumni in your chosen field and put them on your hit list. Most executives like to hire in their own image, and are more likely to be receptive and helpful to graduates of their alma mater.

Find out from the placement office who, in the last few graduating classes, got the kind of job you want, and contact them. Ask them about their company. However, you should go one step further. Ask them about their search and pick their brains for any ideas that could be useful to you in your similar search.

Your Parents' Friends and Contacts: Take full advantage of this type of parental assistance. This is no time for false pride. Don't treat them any differently from the rest of your hit list. Even in the unlikely event that they "give" you an ideal job, because you're somebody's offspring, the day you start working all that will matter is how you perform on the job, not how you got the job in the first place.

Placing an Ad: Even if you can afford to place an "Entry Level Position in _____ Wanted" ad in an appropriate industry publication, it's most unlikely to produce any tangible results. Remember basic supply and demand theory from Economics 101? There are just too many qualified entry level job seekers for good companies to even consider looking at "Situation Wanted" ads. If you're not convinced, find some "entry level position wanted" ads, and contact the people who placed them. Ask what kind of response they received. Don't be surprised if you're unable to find these ads. There's a good reason they're scarce; they don't succeed.

Executive Recruiters: Quality companies very rarely use executive recruiters to fill entry level positions. They pay recruiters up to 35 percent of first year's compensation to find quality people with specific kinds of experience. Again, there are just too many qualified candidates available to justify paying a recruiter. Consequently, executive recruiters are rarely worth your time contacting at this stage of your career. If a recruiter contacts you about a job, treat the recruiter just like a potential employer. Pursue the job if it's on target. If the job fails to satisfy your essential criteria, tell the recruiter why. Ask the recruiter for advice to help you find what you want. Ask if they ever get searches for what you're looking for. At the very least, try to refer the recruiter to a couple of candidates who are on target for the search that you were originally called about. Any good recruiter will note your helpfulness and may contact you in the future with a great opportunity, if you stay in touch. Therefore, make certain that you get the recruiter's name, firm name, address, and phone number. Once you finally land a job, let the recruiter know where you are.

By the way, executive recruiters are paid exclusively by the hiring company. If a "recruiter" calls you and wants *you* to pay a fee, you should run away as fast as possible. No matter what you are promised, they won't teach you anything worthwhile that's not in this book. If they "guarantee" you the job that you want, but for a fee, they're not being honest with you. By the way, if you contact people who placed "entry level opportunity wanted" ads, you'll find that these "placement" agencies are probably the only responses they received.

Conventions: Most industries have at least one big annual convention, where companies gather to meet with their customers and each other. You can find out when and where they will meet through industry publications, the industry association, or by contacting someone in the industry who doesn't have a job for you but has otherwise befriended you. If you're able to attend the meeting, take a hundred résumés with you and go from booth to booth, speaking with someone from every company that meets your criteria. Make certain that you ask for their business cards, so you can follow up with them. Give each person a copy of your résumé. You must be considerate of the fact that they're there to meet with their customers and to conduct industry business. However, the right combination of aggressiveness and politeness will make you stand out as a real go-getter. You should follow up each conversation that interests you with a letter, which I'll cover in Chapter Five, "Showtime: Playing the Interview Game to Win." You should definitely get a convention directory while you're there. It will be the most up-to-date listing of current names and titles. In terms of dress code, you should dress for conventions just as you would for an interview. Even if the dress code for the convention is casual, you're on a job interview, so you had better dress the part.

In-Person Cold Call: If you have a target city, and if you can accept face-to-face rejection, this can be an extremely effective strategy. When one of my closest friends graduated from college in 1972, he didn't get into a graduate program that he wanted. He decided that he wanted to work in New York City. Armed with his résumés, a good suit, well-shined shoes, and his personality, he started walking into reception areas of Fortune 500 companies. At most offices nobody was available to see him. Most of them referred him to Personnel, where he was asked to fill out an "application for employment." However, one company was so impressed with his initiative and style that they made him an offer. He started the following Monday as a management trainee at Time Inc., where he worked for a year before going back to school for his MBA, and subsequently started a very successful career on Wall Street.

Career Seminar: Another aggressive strategy is to sponsor a career seminar in the field that you have chosen. Let's say that you want to get into account management in advertising. Contact an advertising agency near your school. Invite someone from account management to come speak to your school's Advertising Club, which either you will create with other interested students, or if one exists, you'll volunteer to make the contacts and the arrangements. Ask the person you contact to come to your campus to address your club about how to break into advertising and join a follow-up question and answer session. Most executives really enjoy going back to college campuses and will be delighted to accommodate you.

As the contact person, you will have a fabulous opportunity to build a relationship that can result in worthwhile referrals and even interviews. Should you be able to arrange several career seminars with people from different companies, so much the better. Depending on where your school is located, contacting people from industry/trade associations and industry publications can be similarly effective. Also, just because your school is located "too far away," keep in mind that executives travel. An open-ended invitation may even result in somebody rearranging his or her travel schedule to meet with your group. The bottom line is that the career seminar tactic can be a highly effective, and informative, strategy that is well worth the effort and initiative. In fact, it's because of the recognition of your initiative that this approach so often results in interviews.

Internships: If you're lucky (and smart) enough to find an internship in the field you've chosen, it's a fabulous opportunity that you should take advantage of. Aside from the value of the exposure, learning experience, industry contacts, and impressive résumé material, some companies look at internships as a low-risk way to evaluate undergraduates for full-time employment. Some companies even offer intern programs for recent grads. While the short-term compensation is minimal, the medium- and long-term benefits are substantial. To find out about internships, start with your school placement office, professors in your chosen field, and the appropriate industry association.

The concept of internship can be a shrewd way of exploring a career. When I graduated from college, a good friend of mine was uncertain about what she wanted to do after graduation. She thought she wanted to be a lawyer but was concerned about spending three years in law school and discovering that she didn't want to practice law. She came upon the solution of becoming a paralegal for a year. She then attended law school with both solid real-world experience and the confidence that she really wanted to be an attorney.

For making cold calls, for on-campus interviews, when working conventions, and generally for interviews arranged by friends and contacts that you and your parents have, you only need a résumé. But for the hundreds of other companies on your hit list, you need a vehicle to deliver your résumé in a manner that will maximize the number of interview opportunities you receive.

My industry is replete with incredible stories about how people have tried, and occasionally succeeded, to obtain an interview with outlandish stunts. One man, whose written request for an interview had been rejected three times, then called three times with the same lack of success. Finally one morning he lay down behind the car of the CEO, who was trying to leave home for work. The hopeful candidate announced, "I won't get up until you promise me an interview." "I'll be right back," replied the CEO. Five minutes later the police arrived to handle the "lunatic," and the CEO was on his way to the office.

In general, these outlandish tactics will fail, and are rarely worth the expense, both in terms of time and money. My advice is to develop an excellent cover letter that can complement your résumé and favorably distinguish you from your competition. Most of your competition, at least those savvy enough to be launching a direct mail campaign, will merely go through the motions and send pedestrian cover letters. While the wording varies, the takeaway is always the same: "Dear potential employer, *please give me* an entry level job, and please contact me soon because I am desperately seeking a job." Your letter will be different in every meaningful way. Let's get to it and develop a cover letter that's every bit as good as your résumé.

Cover Letters

Letterhead: Ideally, if you can afford it, printed stationery is a big plus. Nothing fancy, black printed on off-white paper, with your name, address, and phone number. The envelope should also be imprinted with your name and address, but no phone number. You'll need standard #10 envelopes, so that your résumé will fit neatly inside. Personally, I prefer stationery that's smaller than the résumé. You'll find that $5\frac{1}{2}'' \times 8\frac{1}{2}''$ is both the most economical and very serviceable. I would recommend that you order at least five hundred of each.

Objective: The only objective of a cover letter (and résumé) is to obtain an interview for a job, no more, no less.

Tone: While it's true that you're seeking employment, your focus must be from the companies' point of view—in other words, what's in it for them. If they have entry level programs and if your background is acceptable to them, you might solve one of their problems by filling one of their entry level openings. The key is to stress the *benefit* to them. Even if they don't have entry level positions, they might make an exception for you if they are shown that there's something in it for the company. Instead of pleading for an interview, your letter will focus on how the company could benefit from your services.

Formality: Starting with your cover letter, and continuing through phone calls and interviews, it is difficult to err on the side of formality. Always use Mr., Ms., or Mrs., until asked to call someone by his or her first name. Once requested, follow their instructions. Personally, I wouldn't make the mistake of asking if it's okay to use a first name. People are well aware of how you're addressing them. Let them decide when it's appropriate for you to be on a first-name basis with them. Rank does have its privileges; make certain that you show the proper respect.

Years ago I had an interview arranged for me by a recruiter. I went to the hotel where the president of the company with whom I was interviewing was staying. As instructed, I called his room at 5:30 P.M. He answered the phone and I said, "Good afternoon, Bill. It's Matt Gordon. I'm in the lobby and available at your convenience." He replied, "I'll be right down, *Mr.* Gordon." His European accent told me right away that I'd blown it; Europeans tend to be very formal in their business dealings. I tried every social skill I knew, including properly extending my pinky as we had tea. Unfortunately, I was hardly surprised to learn from the recruiter that while "Bill" was truly impressed with my background, he felt the chemistry was wrong. It was a lesson I never forgot. Don't ever risk losing an opportunity like that by doing or saying something stupid.

Now let's look at three excellent cover letters (pages 42–44).

All three letters sound like they were written by contributors, not just another job applicant. Each projects commitment, maturity, and a sense that the person is interesting. Let's take Gail's letter and dissect it to understand why it's effective.

The first paragraph addresses benefits that you can expect based on an actual, relevant accomplishment. The second paragraph provides support and specifics. Obviously, Gail is able to discuss *how* she achieved these results, but you'd have to talk to her to find out. The final paragraph states her objective. It demonstrates focus, direction, and conviction. In all, just over one hundred words. It's succinct, flows logically, and says that this is a successful person who knows what she wants and is definitely worth seeing.

In my experience, most people really struggle with their benefit statement. It often takes a lot of thinking about your accomplishments to date as they relate to landing your first job. Maybe you started your own small business at some point. Even if it failed, you probably learned several valuable lessons. Perhaps you had a "McJob" but suggested something that reduced costs or saved time. Maybe you sold advertising for the yearbook or school paper and exceeded last year's sales by 21 percent. Your résumé should help focus your thinking here. Hardly anybody graduates from college without a single worthwhile accomplishment. Once you know what it is, the key is to *merchandise it as a benefit.*

Gail Barker

27 Elm Street #10A
Champaign, IL 61820

217-335-5253

Today's Date

Mr. Robert Fichtel
Vice President Sales
The Palm Company, Inc.
100 Corporate Way
New York, N.Y. 10016

Dear Mr. Fichtel,

Could your sales department benefit from an entry level sales person who averaged +32% annual sales increases the last three summers as a Good Humor Truck Route Salesperson?

While I initially took the job with Good Humor because of the income potential to help finance my education, I quickly fell in love with selling. I created a unique plan (according to my district manager) to achieve these results.

My objective is to find an entry level opportunity in sales where I can learn quickly and advance into sales management based upon the results that I achieve. I know that I could do an excellent job for you.

Sincerely,

Gail Barker
encl.

Robert Jones

170 Frankie Way
New Haven, CT 06513

203-248-1569

Today's Date

Mr. Gary Carter
President
Spalding Publishing
451 Michigan Ave.
Chicago, IL 61001

Dear Mr. Carter,

Could your publishing house benefit from an entry level assistant editor with the equivalent of almost one year of real-world experience? My internship at *Dental News* has solidified both my desire and my confidence to be successful in the publishing business.

While I know that I still have a lot to learn, I am confident that based on my experience I can contribute while I continue to learn. Given the opportunity, I know I could do an excellent job for you.

Sincerely,

Robert Jones
encl.

John Newman

28900 Cortez Ave. #7
San Jose, CA 94016

408-974-9634

Today's date

Mr. David Soman
Commissioner
Calif. Fish & Game Commission
200 Center Street
Sacramento, CA 92431

Dear Commissioner Soman,

Ever since I went snorkeling in Hawaii in 1985 I've dedicated myself to becoming a marine biologist. Perhaps you remember the paper I delivered last October at the MBRA: "The Effect of Acid Rain on Freshwater Shrimp Larvae."

I'm looking for an entry level opportunity in marine biology research. If you have a need I know I could do an excellent job. May we talk?

Sincerely,

John Newman
encl.

If you played varsity sports, you have teamwork experience. If you were ever captain, you have leadership experience as well. Think about what you've accomplished that you're proud of. Most of the time, the same skills you used for that accomplishment can translate into skills that would benefit an employer.

Never Never Land Revisited: Most people would look at this cover letter and say that it's good, but there are several things missing. You'll find the following on a typical job applicant's cover letter, but they should never, never land on yours.

As discussed in Chapter Two, self-evaluative phrases like "bright," "quick study," "energetic," and the like are presumptive at best. Sure, you must eventually display these attributes, but the key is that they're perceived by your potential employer. Let your cover letter and résumé foreshadow your excellent attributes. You'll solidify them face-to-face, in the interview process. In short, job applicants tell you how good they are, job winners simply demonstrate it.

"Résumé attached" statements are covered simply with "encl." (for enclosure) right below your name. Any other references to your résumé just get in the way of what you have to say and the image that you want to convey. If your cover letter doesn't make it clear that you're looking for a job, then you need to rewrite your cover letter. In short, "attached for your consideration is my résumé" kinds of statements are unnecessary clutter, and only detract from the focus of your benefit to them in your cover letter.

Compensation goals should *never, never* be included in a cover letter for an entry level job. As discussed in Chapter One, compensation should not even be a significant consideration in landing your first job. Including it in your cover letter could signal a prospective employer that you're more interested in a paycheck than in an opportunity. Raising compensation objectives can only either screen you out, because you're too expensive, or result in a lower offer than you would have gotten, because you indicated that you'd take less than they were prepared to pay. Compensation isn't really an issue at all until someone is ready to make you an offer. (I'll cover compensation issues in Chapter Five, "Showtime.")

"I'll call you on Wednesday, March 5, at 10:00 A.M. to ..." exemplifies another phrase that should not find its way onto your cover letter. Promising to call on a certain date, or at all, is unnecessary. Nothing in your cover letter suggests that you won't call, so all of your options are open. The ideal situation is to have that person read your letter and résumé, and then pick up the phone to call you for an interview. Why muddy the waters? The next best case is that when you call, an interview is arranged. I'll cover exactly when and how to make follow-up calls later in this chapter.

That covers the basic guidelines for what you should include and what you should omit in your cover letter. A persuasive cover letter and résumé in tandem can help distinguish you from your competition and create more interviewing opportunities. Then it's up to you and your interviewing skills to generate the offer that's right for you.

Cover Letter Options: If you have, or have access to, a word processor, you might consider customizing your initial sentence to include the actual name of the company that you're approaching.

If you have a targeted location and plan to be there in the near future, the following tactic can be very effective. Put a "P.S." on your cover letter that says: "I plan to be in the Metro New York area the week of March 17th." Again, no promise on your part to call, but you have created a sense of immediacy and purpose. Mail the letters one month before your trip. Call everyone who doesn't respond in two weeks and say: "I'm following up on my letter of February 17th, regarding an entry level opportunity in _____. I'll be in town the week of March 17th. When would be a convenient time for you to see me?" Now, be quiet and listen. You've presented the opportunity and have asked for the interview. Let the person respond. If you're told by the person that you're calling, or his or her secretary, that you have contacted the wrong person, find out the name and the title of the right person to contact. Ask: "Did you pass my letter and résumé along?" Whether or not your letter and résumé were forwarded, ask to be transferred to the right person and *ask for the interview.*

Follow-up Calls: Two weeks after your hit list mailing, you will have gotten most of the responses that your mailing will generate by itself. To maximize the benefits of your mailing, you should follow up with everyone who doesn't respond. These calls should have two sequential objectives. Your primary objective is to generate an interview at that company. If the person you wrote to forwarded your letter to someone else, track that person down. The on-the-phone image that will create the most interviews is being courteous, enthusiastic, and slightly aggressive. Never display a lack of self-confidence by responding to a turndown with "what's wrong with me, my résumé, my background, etc.?"

If you can't get an interview, try for objective number two: Ask, "Whom do you know (people or companies) that would be interested in someone like me for an entry level job in brand management? . . . Who else?" When I ran my executive recruiting business, I did this same kind of networking when I searched for candidates. I liked to ask "Who else?" until I got two consecutive "Nobody else" responses. I found that asking again after the initial "nobody else" often generated additional leads. Now, turn around and send your cover letter and résumé to these prime referrals. As an aside, even if your initial contact volunteers the use of his or her name in approaching someone, don't bother. Eventually it will come out that your reference doesn't really know you, creating the real danger that you and your approach will be viewed as a sham.

Aggressive Tactics: Let's assume that you got a rejection letter from a company for whom you would really love to work. You have two options, beyond accepting their rejection. First, you might call as if you haven't received their rejection letter. This can be occasionally effective, especially if you can indicate a time span when you will be in their vicinity and available, which is what you would convey as the purpose of your call. Second, consider approaching some-one else in the company. Try human resources, or even the president. You might even supplement your cover letter with one sentence explaining why the company is your *first* choice. It's human nature to respond positively to someone who likes you. Your statement of endearment must not be contrived. Ide-ally, it should relate to a recent and significant success of that company. I know of people who were rejected by one or two different people in a company, but kept approaching people until they found someone who ultimately sponsored them for a first job.

Another tactic is to wait two or three months and simply resend your cover letter and résumé as if you'd never ap-proached them. Companies' staffing needs change constantly, and these days hiring freezes come and go; timing can be almost everything.

Finally, among your rejection letters will be some sincere compliments, with such phrases as "I was very impressed," or "I wish we had an entry level program." Comb through your rejection letters and call these people. Thank them for their response and seek their help. Restate your objective and ask for advice and referrals. I know people who have done this and gotten great leads or even interviews, and ultimately jobs with the company that originally sent them the rejection letter.

The Hidden Job Market: Learn the value of public relations by hiring a dedicated, hardworking PR person—yourself. The price is right, and what you lack in experience, you'll more than make up for with desire. In addition to the strategies that I've already dis-cussed, make certain that *everyone* you speak with knows that you're looking for an entry level job in_____. Never as-sume someone can't be helpful. For example, when you're home from school and talk with your parents' friends, or your friends' parents, tell them what your objective is, then listen. If you're traveling and start a conversation with a stranger, tell that per-son what you're looking for. You certainly won't do yourself any harm. In short, the more lines that you have in the water, the more likely you are to land the big one!

Interview Generation Summary

1 ▪ School Placement Office	The best place to start
2 ▪ Direct Mail Campaign	The most work and most effective
3 ▪ Alumni Networking	Very effective and often fun
4 ▪ Hidden Job Market	Easy and often effective
5 ▪ Industry Conventions	Fun, interesting, and very effective
6 ▪ In-Person Cold Call	Not right for everyone, but powerful
7 ▪ "Career Seminars"	Very effective, great experience
8 ▪ Public Relations Campaign	A "must" piece of your game plan
9 ▪ Answering Ads	Great *if* you happen to find one that's appropriate

---

There you have it, plenty of ideas, tactics, and strategies for generating interviews. From a time standpoint, the most time-consuming portion of your job search will be over once you complete your direct mail campaign.

The first real-world lesson that salespeople are taught is: You plan your work, then you work your plan. The same adage holds true for job hunting where you're selling yourself.

Chapter Four

Interview Preparation

Prepared Candidates Get More Job Offers

Vince Lombardi would repeatedly tell his NFL champion Green Bay Packers: "Gentlemen, if you fail to prepare, then you are preparing to fail." When it comes to interviewing, nothing could be more accurate. Don't tell me that you don't interview well. Nobody is born knowing how to interview. It's a skill that you must learn, develop, and hone, until it reaches excellence. Throughout your career, you can expect, on average, to make at least three "career leveraging" moves to different companies. To make certain that these moves really exert a positive thrust on your career, it will be just as vital that you interview well as it is that you have established a solid track record of accomplishments.

Now that you understand the importance of interviewing well, I want you to understand the tremendous advantage of being totally prepared. Beyond avoiding wasting precious interviewing opportunities refining your interviewing skills, you will have a tremendous advantage over most of your competition.

It's a fact that even seasoned corporate executives research a company that they're interviewing with less than 5 percent of the time. Well-prepared candidates frequently get offers that better-qualified candidates who don't bother to prepare do not. Less than 10 percent of candidates are astute enough to ask good questions about the company.

I want you to think about interviews as if each interview were the NCAA Final of a sport in which you're a star participant. What we're going to cover in this chapter is what your practices would cover leading up to the Big Game. We have several basic skills to work on, a little window dressing, and by now everybody knows that we'll have a few well-designed trick plays to use when they're least expected. It's work ethic time.

As soon as you have an interview arranged with a company, you must start researching that company. You want to learn as much as you can about their products, financials, culture, problems, and opportunities. There are several reasons why you must do this research. First of all, most of your competition won't bother to spend the time, which will result in your appearing more ambitious, brighter, more mature, and significantly more enthusiastic than those who go in and "wing it on personality." Since you will have more insights than your competition, both your questions and your responses will be both more knowledgeable and more on target. In short, prepared candidates get more and better offers. Unprepared candidates rarely get offers. In addition, if you're ultimately going to accept an offer from a company, don't you want to know as much as possible about the organization you're joining?

By the way, if you and your friends are interviewing with the same companies, regardless of career discipline (i.e. marketing, finance, R&D, etc.), it's often helpful to pool your research efforts in a team approach. Not only is "pooling" a great time saver and more fun, but the ensuing discussion will result in a better understanding of the company.

If researching each company with whom you have an interview scheduled sounds like a lot of work, that's because it is. But when you consider how much work goes into each interview that you generate, you realize how valuable each interview is.

Simply put, either you spend the time researching for your interviews, or you'll probably have to regress back to the interview-generation stage of the job-hunting process. In addition, if you look at it as a worthwhile learning adventure, it can be fun and interesting.

Basic Research: Most companies with whom you interview will probably be publicly held. That means that an annual report will be readily obtainable. Some companies will even send you a "starter" package of information prior to your interview. This will typically include an annual report, the house organ (in-house magazine), and maybe a brochure or two. There may even be a reprint of a recent article about the company that was published in a major business magazine or newspaper. Even if a company sends you an information package, you'll still need to do some research on your own. They *expect* you to read what they send you, and you should recognize that most of your competition will read what they've been spoon-fed. Remember, you're preparing for the Big Game. If you want to be a winner, you must put in that extra preparation.

Annual Report: This is the best place to start to get an overview of the company, and some beginning insights. If they don't send you a copy, one should be readily available through any stockbroker (a service usually reserved for customers) or any good library. You can always get your own copy by calling the company's investor relations department and asking them to mail you a copy. If you call, ask them to include a 10K report and any brochures they have available as well.

In addition to the financials, which you should study thoroughly, there will be a letter to the shareholders from the chairman/CEO. This letter will usually address major problems, opportunities, successes, direction, and corporate philosophy. The five-year P&L will tell you what sales and profits have been. Look for differences in percentage changes from year to year. Look at the internals (all the cost areas below the Sales number and above the Profit/(Loss) number). Are they spending more or less on advertising, R&D, etc.? Pay close attention to the footnotes to the financials; that's where the skeletons are usually buried. The 10K will give you, among other things, an interesting insight into compensation packages for the corporate "elite." Just scouring the annual report by itself, and then thinking about what you have read, will put you dramatically ahead of most of your competition.

Business Periodicals: In addition to any industry-specific publications (like *Advertising Age* for advertising agencies or consumer marketing companies), your research should include the general business publications like *Fortune, Business Week, Barron's, The Wall Street Journal,* etc. They all have periodic "historical indexes." Check for any articles from the last year or so. You'll have to check the regular indexes for any publications not covered by the most recent periodic historical index. Read all the articles that you can find. Take careful notes and place everything worthwhile into one of two categories:

1 ▪ Insights you hope to casually "drop" into your answers during your interview. These should be positives about the company.

2 ▪ Questions about the company, or their business, that you would like them to answer.

Remember, your objective is to demonstrate that you've done your research and have spent time thinking about the company. Never broach a subject if "you're sure" the company is doing something wrong and you know the right way to do it. Even if you're right, what if the person you're interviewing with is responsible for the mistake in the first place? This approach is never well received from a "wet behind the ears student" who is looking for a first job. It's fine to ask "why" a company is doing, or not doing, something. But you might be opening Pandora's box, because after their response, it's fair game to ask you: "What do you think?" Then you'll have to comment.

Once you review any literature they send you, comb through the annual report, and properly research the appropriate business periodicals, your research efforts will easily put you in the top 5 percent of your competition. You've done well, except we're talking about the Big Game. If you really want to win the NCAA Championship, you'll have to do better. Let's think about a trick play.

Guerrilla Warfare: A rarely used, but savvy, approach to gaining valuable insights into a company and its culture is to make a "cold" phone call to someone in the functional department (i.e., sales, finance, etc.) of the company with which you have an interview scheduled. Ideally, you can locate someone with about two years of experience, which should provide you with the most relevant information for your purposes. You may even luck out and have already found an alumnus of your school when you were developing your hit list.

Call the company switchboard and ask to be connected to the head of the functional department that you're interviewing for. When that person, or a secretary, answers the phone, introduce yourself as a college student working on a project. If you're more comfortable using an alias, you should do so. Ask, "Whom could I talk to for five or ten minutes, who could answer a few nonproprietary questions for my project?" Indicate that ideally you'd like to speak with someone who has been out of school for a couple of years. Needless to say, you should be very polite and verbalize your appreciation of their assistance.

Once you get the right person on the phone, you should identify yourself, state the purpose of your call, promise confidentiality, and start right in on your five key questions. Let me share with you the script that I used when I was looking for my first job. "Hi. My name is Matt Gordon. I'm an MBA working on a project concerning how different corporate cultures impact their marketing programs. If you have a few minutes, I'd like to ask you five questions. I assure you that your answers will be both confidential and anonymous. Would now be a good time?"

If the response is "not now," simply find out when would be a convenient time and call back then.

The Five Questions

1 ▪ *How would you describe the corporate culture of your company?* (structured or unstructured, formal or informal, conservative or aggressive, sales driven or marketing driven, product driven or service driven)

2 ▪ *What are the key reasons that people succeed and get promoted at your company?* (tangible accomplishments, seniority, politics)

3 ▪ *What are the reasons that people fail, and even get fired at your company?* (chemistry, failure to produce, politics)

4 ▪ *What do you like best about your job and your company?*

5 ▪ *What do you like least about your job and your company?*

Listen carefully to each answer and take good notes. If you don't understand something, ask for clarification. Under the first three questions, in parentheses, I have included some words to "trigger" their responses, *if necessary.* Don't volunteer the "triggers" unless they ask you what you mean. After their last response, if the conversation has been cordial, you might ask: "Is there anything else that you would like to add?" You never know what extra gems of knowledge you might uncover. Thank them for both their time and their helpful comments. When you hang up, go over your notes and start thinking about what you have learned. Granted, it's only one opinion. However, you were directed to a person who is expected to be representative of that department at that level. At the very least, it gives you added direction when you interview. In the best case, which will be most of the time, you will have keen insights in a league way above and beyond your competition.

You may wonder why I used my real name. In retrospect, not only was there no risk, but a potential hidden benefit. First of all, it's unlikely that the person you call will be on your interview schedule. Even if that person is on your interview schedule, someone with a couple of years of experience is highly unlikely to be a "voting member" of the interviewing team.

At H. J. Heinz, where I got my first job, I ended up being taken out to lunch by the associate product manager I had "cold called." I didn't bring up our prior phone conversation, and he didn't even allude to it, until after lunch. Finally he said, "You know, when I saw your name on the interview schedule, I thought that your name sounded familiar, but I couldn't place it. Once we started talking and I heard your voice, it clicked. As you've probably guessed, my vote doesn't count, but I want you to know that I think what you did was very smart. It demonstrates several good qualities. I hope we're smart enough to offer you a job, and I hope that you take it." The bottom line is that intelligent extra effort is almost always appreciated (and rewarded).

Once you're considering an offer, or deciding between multiple offers and want additional insights, use the same "cold call" technique to the company's direct competition. In this case you're looking for the most senior person possible in the department. Explain that you're a student considering an entry level job with_____(their competitor), and you would appreciate their perspective on your five questions in order to make an intelligent decision. Not only will you receive some additional worthwhile insights, but I know of cases where this strategy has resulted in a request for a résumé, and subsequently an interview and a job offer.

Another useful tactic, under "Guerrilla Warfare," is to do a little firsthand market research about the company's products at retail. If it's a consumer products company, go to major chain outlets, like drugstores, grocery stores, mass merchandisers, hardware stores, home centers, etc., and ask the appropriate section manager of that store about the company's product(s), and about those with whom they compete. Let's say you're interviewing with an auto manufacturer. Go to a couple of their showrooms and also check out their competition. If you're interviewing with an oil company, go to a couple of their gas stations, and to their competitors' gas stations. Ask the owner or the manager about the pluses and minuses. I think you get the idea.

Now that you're properly armed with insights and knowledge way beyond your competition, is there any way that you could still lose the Big Game? Absolutely, because you lack Big Game Experience. It's time to plan your pre–Big Game scrimmages.

Interviewing Practice: No matter how knowledgeable you are about the company, *you must practice your basic interviewing skills* before you actually interview. Without solid interviewing skills, all your work in generating the interview and researching the company is likely to be wasted. When I was looking for my first job, my first eight interviews resulted in rejection. I panicked a little, and started accepting interviews from anyone, even companies for whom I didn't want to work. All of a sudden, everyone with whom I interviewed was making me an offer. Was I suddenly a more valuable commodity? Absolutely not. It's just that through trial and error I'd finally learned the interview game. There's no need for you to waste any precious interviews "learning to interview." The time to practice is *before* your first interview.

Once you have started a "job-hunting team," you can practice as a group. You'll find that the group's constructive criticism will be helpful to everyone. If you don't have a group, start one. Get a friend who is also job hunting for your practice sessions. There are three roles: interviewer, interviewee, and critiquer. You should take advantage of the different lessons you can learn as you role-play each part. Some people find it helpful to tape-record, or even videotape, these practice sessions. You'll be amazed at how different your responses sound on tape. I promise you that once you review your mock interview on tape, you'll agree with the need to practice. As you practice your mock interviews over and over, you will notice how much better and more natural your responses become. That's the whole idea! You want to be able to *listen* during the interview, rather than trying to think about what you're going to say next.

The next chapter, "Showtime: Playing the Interview Game to Win," will give you a laundry list of interview questions you can expect, along with the accepted wisdom regarding the "right" answer. Keep working on the questions that you or your group think are giving you trouble. Also, some people find these practice sessions are most productive when they actually dress in their interviewing outfit. If it works for you, go for it.

Your Questions for the Company: I told you earlier that less than 5 percent of candidates ask questions. They're missing a major opportunity, because a sharp interviewer will evaluate a candidate at least as much by the quality of the questions that he or she asks, as by the quality of his or her responses. It's a rare interview in which the candidate isn't given an opportunity to ask questions. The typical response suggests that most of his or her questions have already been answered, suggesting an unenthusiastic or less than cerebral candidate. Sometimes a candidate will ask a few of what I call "pedestrian questions": What do you like/dislike about working here? Where can I expect to be in three or five years? Or (worst case), How many weeks of vacation would I get? Fortunately, you'll be much smarter and better prepared.

Your research will uncover at least a couple of company-specific questions that you will want to ask. In general, you want your questions to indicate both knowledge about the company (demonstrating that you've done your homework) and enthusiastic interest in joining them. You should make a list of your questions before you leave for your interview. Make certain that they meet the criteria for a good question. With practice, you can naturally preface a question with a lead-in phrase, such as, "I read that very flattering article about your company in *Forbes* last month, and I was wondering ..."

One of my favorite questions for a candidate to ask early is: "What have you done here that you're most proud of?" There are two very positive elements to this question. First of all, it gives the interviewer an opportunity to brag a little, which means that for that part of the interview the interviewer has a nice warm fuzzy feeling. Equally important, it gives you an insight into what is considered a worthwhile accomplishment in that company.

Another solid question area is to ask about the specifics of what you would be doing on a regular daily basis for your first year or so. Another excellent question is to ask what the approval process is for various scenarios (capital expenditures, a cost-saving idea, a new product, advertising copy, package design, promotional programs, etc.). The bottom line is that *you won't go wrong by asking questions related to their business and nitty-gritty questions regarding their operating procedures.* As always, in the job-hunting process, there are pitfalls to avoid.

Never Never Land Revisited, Again: There are several areas that you should not ask about during the interview process. At the top of the list are all questions related to compensation and benefits. After all, you're interested in a career opportunity exclusively at this point. Another area to avoid is asking for preliminary feedback regarding your interview. (In the next chapter I'll give you the "magic question" that will get you this feedback, in addition to some other benefits.) In general, you should avoid any question that is in the realm of what can the company do for you, unless it's mutually beneficial. For example: "I plan to go to night school and get my MBA. Would that be feasible?" However, don't follow up with a question about tuition reimbursement. Save *all* of your benefit and compensation questions until after they make you an offer. The final area to avoid is any question that could be interpreted as showing insecurity on your part. Questions like "What does it take to get fired here?" would typify the kind of questions you should avoid.

Big Game Checklist: You've done your research and studied your findings. You know the company as well as any candidate they have ever interviewed. You've practiced your general interviewing skills to near perfection. It's time to turn your attention to the details, because it's the details that can ruin a perfect and well-practiced game plan.

I'm going to assume that your interview will require you to travel to another city. Your company contact will probably make your travel arrangements. If they're making your hotel reservations as well, make certain that you get the hotel's name, address, and phone number. You'd be amazed at how many Sheratons or Holiday Inns there can be in one city. If someone is meeting your plane, make certain you understand how you'll locate each other. If you are on your own, ask how you should get to the hotel and their office for your interview the next day. (I've seen candidates lose points because they "splurged" on a taxi, instead of taking the hotel's courtesy car.) If it hasn't been made clear, ask specifically what you will need receipts for. If you're on your own, don't have an expensive lobster dinner; you'll appear to be taking advantage of the company.

Your briefcase should be filled with the literature that you've collected on the company and your research notes. You should also bring some extra copies of your résumé, just in case. (You may even meet someone on the plane worth giving a copy to.) Obviously, you'll pack your ticket and your itinerary, and you should, of course, have your prepared question list. Bring along a pad of paper and a couple of pens. Even if you decide not to take notes *during* the interview, you'll want to make notes immediately afterward, while everything is still fresh in your mind.

Consider bringing along appropriate accomplishments that you're proud of. It demonstrates that you're fully prepared to show them what you've already done, and foreshadows what you could do for them. You can be certain that Robert Jones will have reprints of the best articles he edited. John Newman will certainly have copies of his published paper. If you're looking to be a commercial artist, obviously prospective employers will be interested in seeing samples.

Finally, you should have a neatly typed list of your references. In addition to the names, addresses, and phone numbers, your list should clearly indicate when you worked for each person.

Your interview attire should be conservative and business-like. For men, a navy blue business suit with a white shirt, conservative tie, navy or black socks, and well-shined black oxfords is a perfect combination. For women, I recommend a conservative skirted suit or dress, natural-colored hose, and as little makeup as possible. These guidelines are especially appropriate for interviews with Fortune 500 companies. If the career you're pursuing is more on the creative side, your attire may be less conservative. However, when in doubt, you won't go wrong by choosing the more conservative approach within your chosen industry. When it comes to jewelry, nothing too flashy is best, with any engagement ring being the exception. When in doubt about jewelry, don't wear it. Everyone should avoid strong-smelling perfume or after-shave lotion.

Pack your interviewing clothes neatly in a carry-on bag. (For some reason, if you pack your suit in the plastic bags that the cleaner uses it seems to get less wrinkled.) Do not make the mistake of checking your bag. I remember being at Heinz about three months when a candidate spent the day interviewing in blue jeans. It seems the airline sent his bag to Hawaii. We were all told to overlook his attire. He had a perfect résumé, and I liked him a lot. However, he was not offered a job. I've often wondered, if he had used a carry-on bag and had interviewed in a suit, what would have happened?

One final suggestion on precautions. Take along an umbrella, just in case. Why start off your interviewing day with the visual depiction of being all wet? I'd also recommend packing an extra clean shirt and underwear. It's not unheard of to be asked to spend an extra day interviewing.

The final item on your checklist is your appearance. You should have your hair styled in an appropriate corporate hairstyle. If you must keep that beard, it should be neatly trimmed. Your nails should be clean and well groomed. Be sure that your shoes are polished and your clothes are pressed.

Finally, tomorrow is the Big Game. Get yourself psyched up

for it. When I was in school playing basketball, I used to listen to Motown records before games to get myself psyched. I found that the same approach worked for me when it came to getting my adrenaline flowing for an interview. I'm sure you know what works for you. The key is to make certain that you arrive at your interview in the right frame of mind to present yourself as well as possible.

Knowing that you're properly prepared will allow you to take your "nervous energy" and refocus it into enthusiasm. Once you can honestly check off every item on the summary on page 63, you are totally prepared to do your best.

I know that you have stamina to spare. You can party all night and function fine the next day. But whether your Big Game is home or away, you should be in bed by 10:00 P.M., either studying your notes or sleeping. I don't care who you are, interviewing is demanding and mentally exhausting. You need every edge you can get, and a good night's sleep is mandatory if you are to be at your mental peak. Save the partying for another night. Think of how much more fun it will be to celebrate landing the job you want!

P.S. for recreational drug users: Speaking of partying, if you don't already know, at least half of the Fortune 500 companies conduct "drug screens" these days. Some conduct them at the first interview. Others make offers contingent upon passing a drug screen. The irony is that hard drugs, such as cocaine, tend to clear your system in a couple of days. Marijuana, at the other extreme, can take two months of abstention to clear your system to pass a drug screen. I've had candidates practically in tears tell me, "For God's sake, it's not even a felony crime for possession in that state." My response is always the same: "If you want to play their game, you've got to play by their rules. If you want to try to change the rules, go to work for NORML (National Organization for the Reform of Marijuana Laws)." It's your life, but at least you know the ground rules.

Interview Preparation Summary

1 ▪ Practiced interviewing	Essential, frees brain to *listen*
2 ▪ Researched company	*Knowledge* is a big edge
a ▪ Annual report, brochures	Mandatory reading
b ▪ Newspapers, periodicals	Shows some initiative
c ▪ "Cold call" the company	A "secret weapon" for "winners"
d ▪ Check products at retail	A "trick play" for the winning score
3 ▪ List of your questions	Winners are prepared
4 ▪ Briefcase "armed"	Your support materials
a ▪ Research summaries and literature	For a final review
b ▪ List of questions	Frees brain to *listen* and *think*
c ▪ Extra résumés	You may need them
d ▪ Paper and pens	For notes, during or after
e ▪ Writing/art samples	You're already accomplished
f ▪ Reference list	Totally prepared
5 ▪ Suitcase packed with interviewing outfit cleaned and pressed	Don't let the details hurt you

Chapter Five

Showtime

Playing the Interview Game to Win

Whenever I start thinking about the realities of interviewing for a job, I'm reminded of the following story. It seems a certain U.S. senator was looking for a new accountant. The first candidate comes in. The senator looks at him and says, "I just have one question. How much is two plus two?" The candidate looks at him and replies, "Four." The senator thanks him and shows him the door. The second candidate talks to the first candidate before his interview. When the second candidate is asked for the sum of two plus two he replies, "Five?" The senator laughs and says "nice try" and shows him the door. The third candidate has done his homework on his prospective employer. The senator asks him, "How much is two plus two?" Without hesitation, the third candidate says, "How much would you like it to be?" He was immediately hired.

There's an important principle here. The "right answer" is determined solely by the interviewer. Two plus two does equal four, unless you're interviewing to be an accountant for a U.S.

senator. It's important to understand this principle for two reasons. First, it should underscore the importance of doing your research thoroughly. Second, the correct answer won't always be the "right answer."

One of the reasons that interviewing is difficult for most people is that both the interviewer and the interviewee should be playing the same two roles during the interview. Both people are simultaneously a potential buyer and a potential seller, only each person's priorities are reversed. You are in the role of being a seller until you get an offer, at which point you become the buyer. The interviewer is initially the buyer, until the company wants to hire you, at which point the interviewer becomes the seller. While both people must simultaneously play both roles, *the bottom line is that if you don't do an excellent job in your sales role, you'll never have the opportunity to be the buyer!* Concentrate on the selling role and get the offer. Then you can don your "buyer's hat," get any remaining questions answered, and resolve any outstanding issues. You can always turn down an offer you receive, but you can't accept an offer you don't receive.

Another reason interviewing can be difficult is that most executives are not great interviewers. They rarely have formal training in interviewing, and they rarely get feedback to improve their skills. The problem is that even though you're selling, you're not in charge of the interview, the interviewer is. Consequently, you must never try to take control of the interview. However, keep in mind that the outcome of the interview is your responsibility. Therefore, you must sell yourself within the framework of answering the questions that you are asked, and by the quality of your questions.

Three years from now, if you're interviewing for another job, you'll have plenty of real-world experience to discuss. Even so, you'll be evaluated on both your ability to do the job and the image that you convey. The reality is that people evaluate image first, and if you pass the image test, they then decide whether you can do the job. Your appearance and behavior are the first areas to be judged. Most interviewers make up their minds about a candidate in the *first five or ten minutes of an inter-*

view! It may not be right, it may not be fair, but first impressions are crucial in an interview.

You want to come across as healthy, well groomed, properly dressed, and well mannered. You need to demonstrate poise, honesty, loyalty, and a positive attitude. You need to convey that you're a leader as well as a solid team player. In short, you want to come off as an interesting, curious person, with youthful enthusiasm, who would be a favorable reflection both inside the company and outside as a company representative.

Your interview begins as soon as you arrive at the appointed place. If you're late by even five minutes, you may have already blown the interview. You should walk in the door five to ten minutes before your scheduled time. Be courteous and friendly to *everybody*. I don't know if it's true, but it is widely accepted that Procter & Gamble's "receptionists" are degreed psychologists, who observe and report back on candidates' behavior in the waiting room. Introduce yourself, say who you're seeing, and explain that you're a few minutes early and would like to use the rest room before you're announced. Check your hair, your clothes, and even your teeth. Wash and dry your hands. It's a real confidence booster to know that you look perfect. Now you're ready. Go back and ask the receptionist to "please" announce you.

Either before you start interviewing, or at some point during the interview process, you may be given an "application for employment" to fill out. Don't make the mistake of treating this too cavalierly by just writing your name and then writing "see attached résumé." While it's true that these applications are usually geared to nonexempt (hourly) positions, it's also an opportunity to demonstrate your respect for details and your ability to follow instructions. Ideally they'll allow you to take it home with you, so you can type the information neatly and mail it back. If you must fill it out there, print neatly, answer all of the questions, and attach a copy of your résumé. While you won't land an offer by filling out an application properly, don't risk getting vetoed by personnel because you showed disrespect for their application form.

It's Showtime: You're prepared, rehearsed, and look terrific, which gives you the ability to listen, because you won't be busy thinking of questions to ask, or what you'll say next. If the interviewer's secretary comes out to escort you back, treat her with the same respect as you would treat an interviewer. When you meet each interviewer, you should smile, look that person straight in the eye, and shake hands firmly. Failure to make and maintain eye contact is the single biggest mistake that most candidates make when it comes to body language. Allow the interviewer to indicate where you should sit. Unless there's a very good reason to sit elsewhere, such as the sun being in your eyes, follow directions. This is not a time to establish independence. If you have a valid reason for wanting to sit elsewhere, state both the request and the reason in a friendly way and *ask permission.* Try to admire or favorably comment on something in the person's office. Something on the wall, a good book you read that you see on the bookshelf, or even the proverbial family snapshot all can make for good ice breakers. *Never* start on a negative, like lousy weather, a bad plane ride, etc. You want your image to be all positive!

At some point, the first person with whom you interview should tell you what your interviewing schedule is going to be. If the information isn't volunteered, you should ask. Also, try to find out a little bit about each person you'll be seeing. As you wind up each interview, also ask that person specifically about the person you'll be seeing next. You'll be amazed at the useful insights. Finally, ask for a business card, so when you write your thank-you letter you'll have the person's correct title and know how to spell their name.

Each interview will have three basic parts, the interviewer's questions, your questions, and the "selling the company" section. Sometimes the interviewer will tell you how he or she is going to structure the three sections. Some interviewers will even give you the choice. Given a choice, you should always ask for their "overview of the company" first, because it adds to your perspective. However, never lose sight of the fact that the interviewer is the boss. No matter how "comfortable" you feel, don't let yourself ever forget that you're selling from the time you enter the front door until you leave the office. There aren't many, but it's the really astute interviewers who put you completely at ease and then find out more than you want them to.

Before I get into specific questions designed to give you problems, and general guidelines for answering questions, let's take a step back and look at the interview from the interviewer's perspective. In addition to my executive recruiting business, I developed and ran a one-day interactive training seminar to teach corporate hiring managers how to hire. There is a thirteen-point checklist that I call "Tricks of the Trade" to help accurately evaluate candidates.

Tricks of the Trade—The Interviewer's Perspective

1 ▪ Create a fair interview environment for accurate evaluation.

2 ▪ *Listen*—By preparing your questions ahead of time, you are able to really listen to and evaluate what the candidate is saying.

3 ▪ Focus in-depth on something "big" that the person has done to evaluate—competency, depth of knowledge, candidate's thought process—and then role-play and evaluate candidate's "style" in a one-on-one business meeting environment.

4 ▪ Nondirective interviewing—When you think a candidate is holding something back, just look the candidate in the eye, nod, put your hands to your mouth and wait for up to thirty seconds. Only the very, very secure will not respond.

5 ▪ Read between the lines. What's the candidate not talking about that he/she should be? Check back when a response is inconsistent with a previous answer.

6 ▪ Evaluate the questions that they ask. Are they relevant, inquisitive, thorough, challenging, etc.? Chances are it's the same way a candidate will attack business issues.

7 ▪ Look for "learners." Winners talk about *why*, not just *what* happened. They learn from experiences and would handle a similar situation differently next time.

8 ▪ Winners have good self-awareness. They have a handle on their strengths and weaknesses. They know how to leverage their strengths and also how to compensate for (and improve) areas where they're not as strong.

9 ▪ Winners are honest. They will admit a mistake and then tell you what they learned from it. They'll also admit when a success was serendipitous.

10 ▪ Winners are positive. They see the glass as half full. While they see problems, they tend to focus on problems as "opportunities."

11 ▪ Honesty Test—Ask: "Tell me how you feel about honesty." Listen and watch. Does the applicant fidget, clear his/her throat, or physically close up? If so, it's a red flag. You should call references and dig deep.

12 ▪ Read body language while you're listening to the candidate.

13 ▪ Use "check-back" questions to confirm consistency.

In my experience, few people are skilled enough at interviewing candidates to consistently and accurately evaluate someone in the usual hour or less of an interview. Consequently, most interviewers seem to rely on a couple of favorite "pet questions" that they believe will guide them in their evaluation. I'm not saying that that's the way it should be, just that that's the way it is. The reality is that most of the people with whom you interview are too busy doing their jobs to find the time to improve their interviewing skills. Through the years, I've collected these gems. The following twenty-one-gun salute contains those questions which would be appropriate to ask someone applying for an entry level job. After each question, I give you directions for the "correct" response. If in your practice sessions you use these twenty-one questions, and specific questions that you and your friends develop based on specifics in your résumé, you're unlikely to be asked a question for which you don't have a strong, rehearsed answer.

1 ▪ *Tell me about yourself.* A superstar will give a terse, under-two-minute, logical presentation without fumbling or asking for clarification.

2 ▪ *What would you change, if you could, in your life's history?* People who want to make changes are unhappy, insecure, and have failed to learn from their mistakes.

3 ▪ *Name the one, two, or three things that ...* Listing responses for exactly the number asked for demonstrates the ability to listen, follow directions, and make decisions.

4 ▪ *What are you most proud of accomplishing?* The answer should be related to the job you are interviewing for in some way. Be prepared to discuss your answer in depth.

5 ▪ *If you could be the person responsible for a past success in our industry, what would it be and why?* Your response should be appropriate for the company and the job function for which you're interviewing. It also demonstrates your depth of knowledge about both the company and the industry (another benefit from doing your research).

6 ▪ *Where do you want to be x years from now?* Your "x-year goal" should be a consistent career path springboarding from the entry level position for which you're interviewing.

7 ▪ *Tell me about your biggest failure.* Winners are risk takers and have a failure to discuss. Their analysis clearly shows that they have learned from it.

8 ■ *What's the biggest challenge that you ever faced, and how did you handle it?* Superstars tend to focus on why things happened, not just what happened. Like everything else, they learn from their experiences and often would handle the situation somewhat differently the next time, because of what they learned.

9 ■ *What's the biggest risk you ever took? Why did you take the risk, and what happened?* The objective here is to determine if you're a savvy risk taker or an undisciplined gambler.

10 ■ *If you were the president of our company, what would you do differently?* People who ask entry level candidates this question believe that it determines if you have "vision" or are otherwise a troublemaker. (In my opinion this is a poor question to ask an entry level candidate.)

11 ■ *How would you describe your management style?* The accepted wisdom is that while you will describe "your" management style you are really describing what you would like your boss's management style to be. (Another case in which doing your research pays off.)

12 ■ *What is your biggest strength/weakness, and tell me about a recent example?* Demonstrates a combination of knowing who you are and your ability to relate what you've done to their business. By the way, the time-tested advice to candidates on identifying a weakness is to take a strength and overplay it: "I can be too much of a perfectionist and can drive some people crazy until we fix things."

13 ■ *What kind(s) of decisions are most difficult for you?* The dual objective here is to discover weaknesses and to learn your thought process for handling difficult decisions.

14 ■ *What interests you least about this job?* Although all jobs have downsides, be careful. While you *must* identify one aspect of the job that isn't terrific, you must indicate a willingness to do the whole job.

15 ▪ *Why should we hire you?* This is a tremendous opportunity to demonstrate both your understanding of the job and how your qualifications match their needs.

16 ▪ *Tell me about a situation in which you were under time pressure and how you handled it.* The twofold objective is to see both what you consider to be a real time pressure situation and how you handled it. (If you don't have a work-related situation, I'll bet that the combination of handling your schoolwork and interviewing for a job created some time pressure situations.)

17 ▪ *Tell me about a problem you had with a peer, and how you solved it.* The objective here is to evaluate your people skills in a nonreport situation, arguably the most difficult people-management situation.

18 ▪ *Whom would you model your career after and why?* You should choose a well-respected person in the same industry. The "why" part of your response will demonstrate your values and aspirations.

19 ▪ *Tell me about the same mistake that you made more than once.* Even superstars occasionally repeat mistakes, but they learned something different each time.

20 ▪ *What question(s) were you afraid I'd ask, but didn't?* This is a security check. There are no questions that you feared.

21 ▪ *What question(s) did you want me to ask that I didn't?* This is intended to give you a chance to talk about anything that you think is important to your candidacy, but haven't had an opportunity to say. The proper response is simply stating the question(s). If the interviewer doesn't probe further, say, "Would you like me to respond, or were you just curious about the questions?"

As you rehearse, practice, and hone your responses and interviewing skills, let me give you some general guidelines:

1 ▪ *Short Answers:* Keep all your responses under two minutes. Longer answers run the very real danger of boring the interviewer. When the interviewer wants to hear more from you, he or she will ask. This avoids making the mistake of rambling on about something that the interviewer isn't interested in.

2 ▪ *Honesty:* Yes, you want to present the best possible "you" that you can. But be yourself. The best job fits are right for both sides. You may be able to play a role for even a full day of interviewing, but it won't take long on the job for the real you to surface.

3 ▪ *Have Fun:* You'll be meeting new people, learning about companies and industries, and taking that monumental first step in your career. It's exciting, demanding, and challenging, but don't forget to enjoy it. Besides, if you're having fun, it can only help you.

4 ▪ *Analyze Your Answers:* Do your answers convey the right image and impression? Is what you're not saying, saying more than what you *are* saying?

5 ▪ *The Black Hole:* Avoid all four known entrances to "The Black Hole of Interviewing:" *politics, race relations, religion,* and *sports.* For every person you turn on, you risk turning off ten. All four areas are a Pandora's box you want to avoid the risk of opening.

In 1982, I was interviewing for a job. Before making an offer, the company I was interviewing with had a policy of using psychological testing. Their psychologist was also the team psychologist for the New York Giants, my favorite football team. After my testing, we got into a discussion regarding whether Phil Simms or Scott Brunner should be the Giants' starting quarterback. I made the statement that I saw, in a then young Phil Simms, the same qualities that I had seen in Terry Bradshaw early in his career. He told me that I was completely wrong, that Phil Simms had nervous feet, and the future was clearly Scott Brunner. While history clearly vindicated my prognostication, the company chose to offer me a different job from the one I had interviewed for, and wanted, based on my "testing" results.

6 ▪ *Body Language:* Personally, I think that reading body language is overrated. Sometimes people just sit in a way that's comfortable. However, some interviewers put a great deal of emphasis on it. Hands in front of mouth indicate a listening mode. Leaning slightly forward in your chair, not fidgeting, *making good eye contact,* and directly facing the interviewer would be considered correct interviewing posture, in terms of body language. My advice is to be cognizant of body language, but not so concerned that it interferes with feeling at ease. I also believe you're much better off listening to what's being said than trying to read your interviewer's body language. However, keep in mind that you're communicating, and good eye contact facilitates communication.

7 ▪ *Illegal Questions:* The legal world relative to employment has become very complex. Often, an interviewer isn't even aware that the question he or she is asking is illegal. (For example, most people are shocked to learn that it's illegal to ask, "How did you learn to speak Spanish?") You really only have one option, if you want the job; just answer the question. Should you opt to "report" the incident, do you really expect them to ultimately offer a job to a troublemaker like you? However, should you find yourself subjected to a couple of abusive illegal questions, or overt sexually abusive behavior, by all means, you should report such unprofessional conduct to either the human resources person with whom you interview or your company contact who invited you out for the interviews. *No candidate should tolerate extreme, abusive behavior.*

8 ▪ *Compensation:* Should you be asked about your compensation expectations, there's only one correct position to take. Refocus the issue on your *sole* concern of finding the right opportunity. Indicate that if they make you an offer, you're confident that it will be fair. However, compensation "will not be a major factor compared to the opportunity." Some people like to take an aggressive posture when asked about compensation expectations. They respond by asking if the company is ready to make them an offer. When told, "not yet," they refocus to discussing opportunity, as I suggested. My advice is to avoid asking if they're ready to make an offer. It's too easy to come off as pompous and arrogant, and you have nothing to gain. Trust me; when the company is ready to make you an offer, they will.

9 ▪ *No Smoking: Never* risk smoking in an interview, even if the person interviewing you smokes. The word will get around that you smoke. While this may be a small positive with other smokers (who are now a minority), it's often a major negative with nonsmokers. Therefore, when you practice interviewing, you should practice not smoking.

10 ▪ *Paint Your Portrait:* You know what kind of an image you want to project, as well as what you "bring to the party." The sum total of your responses should consistently work together to paint the self-portrait that you want the company to see.

The key to successful interviewing is understanding that you should be wearing your "selling shoes" throughout.

Company Overview: This is the interviewer's "sell" portion of the interview. Ideally, it will be done up front. If not, it's likely to be done last. Listen carefully to what is said. If it's your style, pull out a pad and *ask* if it's okay to take notes. (I've never even heard of anyone being told it's not okay.) Look for consistency among the comments from each person with whom you interview. Is this a company with good lines of communication and a common vision, or does it seem like they're working for different companies? Unless asked to interrupt with questions, you should hold your questions until the end. You can learn a lot by not only what they say, but what they don't say. This is the only time before you get an offer that you're wearing your "buyer's hat." But don't forget that you've still got your seller's hat on underneath. What you must understand is that until you've received an offer, you're *always* selling.

Your Questions: This is the situation in the Big Game where you're playing offense and defense at the same time! The fact that you get to ask questions does make you the buyer. But keep in mind that you will be evaluated as much by the quality of the questions that you ask as by the quality of your responses to the interviewer's questions. Fortunately, you're already ahead of almost all of your competition. You walked into the Big Game with a solid list of questions that will accomplish both of your goals: 1) getting the offer, and 2) deciding if you want the job. That's because you'll be getting some of the additional information that you need to decide if they're the right place for you. More important, you planned your questions to impress them.

Throughout their interviewing process, you may develop additional questions. Terrific, just add them to your list. But never lose sight of this important precept: *Your sole objective is to be a successful seller and to get an offer.* You can always turn down an offer. You're in an even better position to ask questions once they've made you an offer and you exclusively become a buyer.

My advice is to start with "What have you done here that you're most proud of?" for the reasons explained earlier. It's informative and creates a good environment for the rest of your questions, which will demonstrate your knowledge (research efforts), enthusiasm, interest (research efforts), and professionalism. A revealing question to ask everybody you interview with is "Where do you see the company heading in the next three to five years?" Listen carefully to what each person says and you'll quickly know if this is a unified company with well-communicated goals or a potential nightmare of a group of people with a common employer but a wide spectrum of individualized agendas.

If you don't get a chance to get all of your questions asked, don't worry about it. That's why you prioritized your list of questions, from the most impressive/important on down. Don't make the mistake of deposing questions from the top of your list of questions that you develop during the interview. Before you ask an extemporaneous question at the interview, make sure it's either about their business, or about procedures that they use to run their business. If it's not, chances are it should go on your list of questions to ask *after* you receive an offer.

Magic Question: Remember your sole objective? If you want an offer, doesn't it make sense to *ask for the job?* You'd be amazed at how few candidates, even enthusiastic ones, ask for the job. You've been selling for the entire interview. Once you've finished your sales presentation, you should close the sale by asking for the job (even if you have doubts about wanting the job). You don't have to accept an offer, but what if your doubts get resolved and you end up really wanting the job? Asking for the job should be your final sales pitch.

There are several different approaches to asking for the job, depending on whether it's the first interview of the day, the third, or the last. You should develop your own phrases, but let me share with you my personal favorites:

"This sounds very exciting. I'd love to be a team member in your company/department."

"This is a terrific organization. I really want this job."

"Your company offers exactly what I want (give specifics). I'd give anything for this opportunity."

If your interview is on campus, or clearly a one-person screening interview, try "What you've described sounds very much on target with what I'm looking for. What are the next steps?"

Once you've asked for the job, listen carefully to the response, because it's all the feedback that you'll get for now. The response may be somewhat noncommittal, but you'll often find at least a hint or two, especially if you came across extremely well. Don't make the mistake of appearing insecure by asking for more feedback than they volunteer. Companies like to offer jobs that will be accepted. You've done everything that you can. You'll just have to wait for them to complete their decision-making process.

The Interviewing Team: If you spend an entire day interviewing at a company, you will interview with as many as six people or more. These people comprise the "interviewing team." Generally you will interview with a cross-section of levels on the corporate hierarchy, and possibly people from different departments. Some people will be nonvoting team members. Some people will fill more than one role on the team. Some companies will tell you the status of some or all of the team members, while others will leave it up to you to guess. Throughout the process, you should treat *everyone* as though he or she could veto your offer. Even the most junior person you meet who announces, "I'm not really supposed to evaluate you," should be treated as the swing vote in your candidacy.

There are only four roles on the interviewing team. Some people will be fulfilling multiple roles. It can only benefit you to understand these roles:

Recruiting Officer: This is the person who was probably your contact in making arrangements for your trip. The recruiting officer coordinated your interview schedule and will handle any problems that arise, such as rescheduling a missed plane flight. Unless you are instructed otherwise, this is the person who will facilitate your reimbursement for any of your out-of-pocket travel expenses. The recruiting officer will be either out of human resources or someone the department head designated. You will usually meet this person first. Normally you will see this person for a second time at the end of your interviewing day for a "wrap-up interview." Therefore, you should wait until this time to ask this person for the job. The recruiting officer is almost always a key voting member of the team.

Hiring Authority: This is the person who has veto power over any candidate. It may be your potential boss's boss, or your potential boss. At the entry level, it often is somebody higher in the organization, maybe even the department head. It's almost always the highest-ranking person with whom you interview.

Voting Members: These would be people like your potential boss or anyone at that level or above, and generally everyone that you meet from other departments. While these people don't usually have veto power, their votes count. I've seen this portion of the team collectively either "kill" a candidate both the hiring authority and the recruiting officer liked, or create an offer for a candidate both the hiring authority and the recruiting officer were ambivalent about. The point is that there are no unimportant members of the interviewing team.

Nonvoting Members: These are people at the level for which you're interviewing, who generally are really on the schedule for your perspective. Like the voting members, they're usually the cream of the department. These people are having their interviewing skills developed and tested. However, their feedback can either hurt you or help you, especially if your candidacy is on the fence.

Wrap-up Interview: At the end of your day you will probably meet again with the recruiting officer for a quick "tell me what you think" and "do you have any questions that weren't answered?" meeting. If your question doesn't meet the criteria of selling your candidacy, it can wait until you get the offer. My advice is to summarize (in under ninety seconds) the positive parts of the opportunity, and disregard any negatives you have discovered. *The logical conclusion to your "opportunity summary" is to ask for the job with conviction.* After whatever feedback you get, you should reiterate your appreciation for the opportunity, and reinforce your enthusiasm by saying that you're looking forward to hearing from them ("because I really want to work here").

Drinks and Meals: Your full day of interviewing will certainly include lunch. You may even have had dinner with someone on the interview team the previous night. Perhaps you'll be asked out for a drink afterward. In any case, it probably won't seem like an interview situation, and you may even be told that it's purely social. *Don't ever stop being a candidate until you are made an offer!* Whether they admit it or not, they're still evaluating. It may even be a formal test of your manners, social skills, and ability to represent the company outside of the office. Certainly for marketing and sales positions, where you will be entertaining customers at some point, it should be a formal test.

Fortunately, the days are gone when you had to prove that you could hold your liquor. If you're not a drinker, don't hold your liquor well, or just want to be smart and play it safe, you should order something nonalcoholic. I strongly advise you to avoid any alcoholic beverages until you have an offer. If you want to risk having a drink, you should ask your host or hostess what they're having. Let's say that they're ordering beer or wine, and you order a martini straight up; you might be seen as marching to a different drummer, maybe even someone with a potential drinking problem. If asked to have another drink you should *always* decline, even if everyone else is having another. If necessary say, "No thanks. One is my limit." Whether you have one drink or none, your objective is to demonstrate prudence and responsibility.

Meals during interviews are generally not the portion of the interview process in which you'll convince somebody that they should offer you the job. However, they are a time when they could well decide not to offer you the job, even though you have come across successfully as somebody who could do the job.

Good manners are a must. When ordering, take the lead from your host or hostess. If you're told to order whatever you want, you should ask what they recommend. Generally, you'll be safe if you order something that doesn't exceed the median price range of the menu or their recommendations. Another important consideration in what you order is deciding how easy it is going to be to eat. You're going to be carrying on a conversation during the meal. Something like ribs is going to be very awkward to handle while you're trying to carry on a conversation.

Another test that you may be taking is your ability to make a decision, so don't linger too long in deciding what to order. This isn't a social occasion; just make a selection based on the criteria I've given you and get back to *selling*. A final meal test to be aware of is never to season your food until you've tasted it. Some people will interpret your seasoning before tasting as indicative of someone who makes snap judgments before gathering the available relevant information.

Finally, I would recommend that you be sure you know what you're ordering. Many years ago, one of my cousins married a very nice guy soon after they graduated from college. He was taken out to lunch by a company with whom he was interviewing, and ordered steak tartare, medium rare. The waiter asked him whether he wanted a hamburger or steak tartare. As he came to understand that steak tartare is seasoned raw ground beef (with a raw egg yolk), he thanked the waiter for warning him and ordered the chopped steak deluxe, medium rare. The happy ending this time was that the company ended up hiring him for his first job. So you see, you *can* survive making a mistake. Never assume that you've blown an interview. Start selling when you enter the front door and don't stop until you walk back out.

Postinterview Tasks: There you are either sitting in your room, or on a plane going back to school, with the interviews you've just had still fresh in your mind. Running the interview gauntlet is grueling, exhilarating, and clearly exhausting. You may think that you've done everything you can to sell your candidacy, but you haven't. You still have a couple of tasks left to complete.

Notes: While everything is still fresh in your mind, you should formalize your notes on the company. Write down everything significant that you have learned about the company and the people you met. Make a list of your unanswered questions. If their process requires another interviewing trip a month or so later, you'll have solid notes to help you prepare, an advantage over most of your competition who will be trying to *remember* which company had which program, problem, or whatever.

Self-evaluation: Once you have finalized your notes you should reflect back on your performance. What did you do well? What could you have done better? Obviously you will want to have more practice sessions to work on the areas in which you think you need improvement.

Thank-You Letter: Your final task is to send a short letter, thanking the people with whom you interviewed. Do not view this in any way as an opportunity to say something about yourself that you forgot to get across during the interview. The interview was the opportunity to sell yourself. Don't make it obvious that you were unable to get a key point across. Besides, if it didn't surface in their formal interviewing process, it's probably not very important, at least to them.

Should you really want the job, take the time to write to each person with whom you met. It's a nice touch if you can personalize each letter with a reference to something that you discussed. Make a point of saying thank you. Indicate why you are excited and enthusiastic about the position/opportunity. When you write your letter to the hiring authority/recruiting officer, close by asking for the job. Any unreimbursed travel expenses should be summarized with receipts and included in the letter to the recruiting officer, or to whomever you were told to submit them. Your letter should be short, a couple of paragraphs at the most. The takeaway from your letter should be, "This is a person with class." Let me give you two examples.

Gail Barker
27 Elm Street #10A
Champaign, IL 61820
217-335-5253

Today's Date

Robert Fichtel
Vice President Sales
The Palm Company, Inc.
100 Corporate Way
New York, N.Y. 10016

Dear Rob, (Mr. Fichtel asked Gail to call him Rob)

   Yesterday was truly a most interesting and exciting day. Thank you for the opportunity to meet with you and the other people in your organization. I was most impressed by both the people I met and the progressive entry level training program that you have developed.
   The bottom line is that I would love the opportunity to join your team. Thanks again for your hospitality. I look forward to hearing from you.

Most sincerely,

Gail Barker

P.S. As you requested, attached are my receipts and my expense summary totaling $47.50:

Expense report summary	
cab to O'Hare with tip	$15.50
courtesy car to hotel tip	1.00
cab to LaGuardia with tip	15.00
cab home from O'Hare with tip	16.00
Total	$47.50

John Newman
28900 Cortez Ave. #7
San Jose, CA 94016
408-974-9634

Today's date

Mr. David Soman
Commissioner
Calif. Fish & Game Commission
200 Center Street
Sacramento, CA 92431

Dear Commissioner Soman,

Thanks again for taking the time to see me even though the current state budgetary crisis has forced you to temporarily place a freeze on new hires. I must admit that I'd give anything to be able to be on your team for that Russian River project; it starts right where my project on acid rain and shrimp larvae concluded.

I really appreciate the lead you gave me for The Crustacean Institute. I'll let you know what happens after I speak with Dr. Lyons.

Most sincerely,

John Newman

P.S. Obviously, if your hiring freeze is lifted I would love the opportunity to be a candidate for the Russian River project.

Chapter Six

All About Offers

How to Time, Handle, Evaluate, and Accept Them

Waiting to hear back from companies about entry level jobs is a lot like your senior year in high school, when you were waiting to hear from colleges—with one major difference. When you apply to college, you get to hear from every school that you apply to before you have to make a decision. Even if you get wait-listed somewhere you would prefer to go, you'll know if you've been accepted or denied in time to enroll there. Unfortunately, you will not find the corporate world as accommodating.

It would be wonderful if you could arrange for all of the companies who are going to give you an offer to do so at the same time. Better yet, why don't they allow until August 1 for all entry level candidates to make a decision? Welcome to the real world. Corporations don't operate on a school-year calendar, unless their fiscal year coincidentally begins on September 1. Because some corporations are beginning their fiscal year each month, even direct competitors can be in different phases of their annual business process at any given time. You must keep in mind that companies are looking to solve their problems, not yours.

Because on-campus interviews are spread out throughout the year, it is even more difficult to "time" your offers together. One way to try to maximize the number of offers that you get at the same time is to have mailed your entire hit list on the same day. If your job-hunting campaign has focused on a single city, and you made a major mailing around a ten-day interviewing trip to that city, you obviously have a better chance of receiving multiple offers on similar timing.

But wait a minute! Are you collecting offers, or are you looking for that *one right job* that meets all of your essential criteria? Never, ever lose sight of your sole objective. If the job you just interviewed for is right on target for you, there may be more that you can do than just wait to hear from them.

Before you left your interview, you asked what the next step was. The matrix of possibilities is simple. Either you were asked to contact them on a given date, or you were told that they would contact you by a given date. You should also know whether the next step is an offer or another interview. If the scenario is another interview, you should know whether that is their usual process, or if you're involved in a "shoot-out" with one or more other candidates.

Their Call: Most companies will leave the ball in their court to contact you. Whenever that date is more than four weeks after your interview, you have an opportunity to gain a further edge over your competition. While your competition is just wasting their time waiting to hear from the company, you'll be busy reinforcing the strength of your candidacy. Write the recruiting officer another letter. The letter should be short and merely reiterate your high level of interest and enthusiasm. Indicate that you're looking forward to hearing from them on whatever timing they indicated. You never know when that one extra step is going to be the tiebreaker between you and another otherwise equal, but less ambitious candidate, for that last open slot.

When you write your "I'm still very excited and interested letter," it's a real plus if you are able to include a "relevant article of interest" that you found in a publication. It doesn't matter if they've already seen the article (they probably have if it's specific to the company). The best article of interest would relate to a topic that surfaced during your interview. More than reinforcing your interest, it proves that you are thinking about them and their business, as if you plan to start working there after you graduate. It also proves that you were listening to what was said during your interview and that you know what's relevant. How could they rationally select another candidate over you, even if you both interviewed well? You've already demonstrated that you have the initiative to go at least one step further.

Your Call: Generally, companies will contact you regarding whether or not they're going to offer you a job. Pragmatically, they don't want to deal with your calls until they've made a decision. Sometimes you'll be told that if you don't hear from them by a specific date, you should give them a call. You must then call them on the timing that they indicated. When you call, the tone in your voice should be enthusiastic, positive, and self-confident. Convince yourself, before you call, that they're going to offer you the job, so that it will be easy to be in the right frame of mind and project a confident image.

Another Interview: Should the company want you to come back for another interview, you'll already know whether that's their process, or if it's a unique situation in which they're making a final decision between you and one or more other candidates. Either way, your game plan for the interview will be the same. In addition to researching the company for articles published since your last interview, you should follow all the same steps outlined on page 63 in Chapter Four, "Interview Preparation." It is paramount that you review your notes from your last interview there. That way you'll be on the same wavelength as the company, and way ahead of your competition who comes in trying to wing it from memory.

You should avoid asking people the same questions you asked them last time; consequently, it may be more difficult to prepare your list of questions to ask. However, the questions that you ask are at least as important at this stage. You know more about the company than you did at your initial interview, so the *quality* of your questions is expected to be better. You should handle the interview day just as you did last time. Obviously, you were on the right track with them or you wouldn't have been asked back. Make certain to end the interview by asking for the job. Needless to say, if the day ends and they still haven't made you an offer, you'll send everybody with whom you met a thank-you letter.

Reversing Rejections: At some point, virtually everybody will experience being rejected for employment. When a company rejects you, you have only two options. If it's a job that you weren't very interested in, for whatever reason, you're better off accepting their decision and devoting your efforts toward those companies which will satisfy your essential criteria. On the other hand, if you're rejected by a company that offers you everything you're looking for, you have a few options that just might end up getting you an offer.

One strategy is to phone the recruiting officer. Express your disappointment, and reiterate that you are still most interested and enthusiastic about working for them. Indicate that you would like to be put on a backup list in case all of their offers aren't accepted, somebody decides later to reject an offer he or she had previously accepted, or the entry level headcount is expanded. Once you have made your interest in being an alternate clear, don't make the mistake of pestering that person with repeated phone calls, which will do you more harm than good. In order to keep your candidacy top-of-mind, follow up with a monthly letter campaign, as I discussed. Again, your letter(s) should be short, interesting, and maybe even humorous.

Another strategy is to call the recruiting officer the day that you receive your rejection letter, as if you are still waiting to hear from the company. Your opening would be along the lines of "You said that I'd be hearing from you by (whenever they indicated). I'm still very excited about the opportunity and was understandably curious as to where you stood on your selection process." Your expectation is that you will end up going to the fallback position of asking to be put on a backup list. However, most people don't like having to tell someone bad news. Maybe you'll get some helpful advice for your job-hunting campaign. You might even receive some useful feedback from your interview. Do not ever make the mistake of asking what you did wrong or could have done better at the interview, because it projects tremendous insecurity. Your objective is to, at least, get on that backup list. Don't do anything to damage the image that you've worked so hard to build. Since you're asking someone to have a conversation with you that he or she preferred to handle with a letter, any feelings of remorse and guilt on his or her part will work in your favor. Win or lose, you should maintain the same interviewing posture that you have all along. You never know whom you'll run into again and under what circumstances. The fact that you're dealing with someone who is successful in the field that you've chosen makes it even more likely that your paths will cross again.

Another strategy to try to reverse an initial rejection is to contact someone else in the company in hopes of finding someone to "sponsor" your candidacy. While this may be someone you met interviewing, you're more likely to be successful with someone new. Take a shot at the president of the company. Send the same cover letter and résumé that you're using for your hit list. Don't mention that you've already interviewed and been rejected. However, you should modify your basic letter to specifically state why that company appeals to you so much. Given what you have learned about this company between your interviews and your research, it should be relatively easy to hit their hot buttons.

The following, more radical, strategy has the best chance of succeeding in a company that doesn't ever, or usually, hire entry level people. If the company really appeals to you, tell them that you're so confident you can produce for them that you would be willing to work for them for free for two or three months, in order to have an opportunity to prove yourself! Obviously, you've either got to really want to work for them, or be getting desperate to use this approach. But if they agree to your "free trial offer," the odds are excellent that it will result in a full-time salaried job. I'm aware of cases in which just making the free trial offer so impressed a hiring authority that he turned around and offered the candidate a salaried position immediately. It clearly tends toward being a drastic measure, but under the right circumstances it can be powerful and very effective. Of all of the strategies that I have suggested to reverse a rejection, the free trial offer is by far the most likely to be successful. However, you must be prepared to work your tail off for a couple of months before they start paying you. Also, no complaining—after all, it was your idea!

None of the other strategies for reversing rejections has a good chance of working. However, if the company really offers you everything that you're looking for, these strategies are worth the effort, *while you continue your job search.* When you think about it, you have a lot going for you. First of all, you're among the very select group of people who made it through their initial screening process and their formal interviewing process. Just because you were "rejected" doesn't mean they weren't impressed with you.

You now have an opportunity to demonstrate your maturity by how you deal with them after you've been rejected. You know that they offer you what you want and that you were awfully close to getting an offer. The company may get more offers rejected than they had expected. Two or three months from now, someone who had accepted an offer may change his or her mind. (Fifteen percent of all employment offers that are accepted ultimately result in the person who accepted the job never going to work for that company.) Finally, headcount changes do occur and a company's entry level needs could increase.

If the unexpected opening does materialize for any reason, your rejection reversal campaign has you ideally positioned as an easy and immediate solution to their problem. You've already been interviewed. All that the company needs to do is to make you an offer, have you accept, and *their problem is solved.* Granted, it's a long shot, but it is a possibility. It will increase your chances, and you have nothing to lose except your "still looking for an entry level job" status.

References: Surprisingly, some companies never request references for entry level positions right out of school. However, you must be prepared to give names and phone numbers of references when you show up for your interview. At an absolute minimum, you should be prepared to give two references. An ideal reference is a supervisor/ boss from a summer or part-time job. Second, you can use professors who know you well. But keep in mind that you're not seeking a job as a student, so if you have two or more business references, use them.

When I ask candidates for references, a red flag that I always look for is a company for whom they have worked, yet haven't listed anyone there as a reference. The most impressive candidates list everyone for whom they have worked (except their current company) and say, "Feel free to call anybody." Not surprisingly, their references are almost always a confirmation that the candidate is terrific.

Think how impressive you will be when you say, "Here is a list of everybody for whom I have worked, summers and part-time, since I started school. I have also included two professors who know me well. Feel free to call anyone." Of course, don't volunteer your references until you're asked for them.

When you do hand over your list of references, in addition to names and phone numbers, it should detail the dates you worked for each person and the company for whom you worked. If you've lost track of someone who would have given you an exceptional reference, you'll learn the valuable lesson about whom you should keep in touch with.

Common courtesy dictates that you ask someone if it's okay to use him or her as a reference, before you give out his or her name. Common sense mandates that you had better check out your references before including them on your list. Tell your potential references about your job hunt. After all, you've already worked for them, and they may offer some unexpected and unrequested assistance. Then *ask* them how they would feel about giving you a reference. Listen carefully to what they say. Are they enthusiastic or merely accommodating? If you're unclear on what kind of a reference they will give you, ask them. Don't assume, just because they respond that they'd be happy to give a reference, that it will be good. Ask, "If you were called as one of my references, what would you say about me?" Don't get argumentative. If you're not happy with what they would say, don't put them on your list. Promise them that if you give out their name and phone number to someone, you will call them as soon as possible and let them know who's going to call them. If they're unavailable when you call back, just leave a message. Also, ask if they would please call you after they've been called as a reference. Ultimately, you should return this courtesy when your job search is successfully completed by sending a thank-you note to each reference for helping you. Besides, you now realize the importance of keeping in touch and maintaining your image with these people.

Most people are delighted to give references, especially for people they like. However, you should make it clear that they will not be besieged by reference calls. Your expectation, and most companies' practice, is that references aren't checked until the company is ready to make an offer. Since you have already checked out your own references, you can be confident that you'll be fine. By the way, don't make the mistake of assuming that someone will give you a bad reference. Call that person and ask. Most people tend to give good or better than deserved references. Bad memories tend to fade, and good memories endure.

I will never forget one time when I was sitting in my boss's office. Our meeting was interrupted so that he could take a phone call to give a reference for someone he had fired for substandard performance. Listening to him, you would have thought that this person was the star of the industry. When I asked him why he had given such a glowing reference for someone he had fired, he said, "He's really a nice guy. I don't want to stand in his way of a good opportunity." The reason I tell you this story is not to delve into a discussion of the morals and ethics of references, but because this is the real world. You should be aware of the fact that few people will give a bad reference. Use this knowledge to your advantage.

Offers—An Overview: Throughout your job search you've had the sole objective of getting *one* offer that meets your essential criteria, and if you're lucky also meets some or all of your desired criteria. However, keep in mind that receiving an offer may place you in the final stretch, but you haven't crossed the finish line yet. First of all, any offer that a company makes to you is a "contingent" offer. At the very least, it's contingent upon your accepting it. They have a legal right to withdraw any unaccepted offer that's on the table. Therefore, in general, the sooner you accept an offer, the better. The offer may also have other conditions attached to it. In addition to requiring that you graduate, typically these could include a drug screening test and/or a medical examination (for insurance purposes).

When you get an offer, make certain that you understand all of its elements. What is the starting salary and benefits package? When is your start date? What will your title be? When will you have your first salary review? Are you included in a bonus program? Now is the time to make certain that all of your questions get answered. Most companies will follow a verbal offer with a written "offer letter." They will probably include a company benefits package. If either the offer letter or the benefits package is not specifically mentioned, you should request them. The roles are clearly changed now. You are definitely the buyer, and your prospective employer is the seller. But even though you have become the buyer, you still don't hold all of the cards. I've seen candidates get offers they really wanted, don their buyer's hat, and behave in a manner that bought them a rescinded offer! *Remember that you must continue to demonstrate that you are the same fine person they want to hire.*

Negotiating Offers: Especially at the entry level, by and large, you should consider all offers to be nonnegotiable, with two small exceptions. One of the elements of the offer will be your start date. Depending on their entry level training program, they may or may not be flexible on your start date. If you would like to start either sooner or later than the start date given, you should *ask* if it would be possible to start on a different date instead. I would also counsel you to share the reason. I've seen even rigidly structured entry level programs make an exception on start date for a variety of worthwhile reasons. Make certain that both your carefully chosen words and your tone make it clear that this is a request, not a demand.

Even if you have plans to spend the summer in Europe after graduation, and will reject their offer if they can't change your start date from July 1 to September 1, you should ask if it would be possible. Should the company be either unable or unwilling to accommodate your desired start date, then you will have to decide whether or not to accept the offer. If you decide to reject an offer because their start date is unacceptable, explain nicely why you are rejecting the offer. Once they understand why, they *may* decide to accommodate you. If not, at least you didn't burn a bridge there. Keep in mind, once you reject an offer you should consider it history.

The only other element of the offer that you should even consider negotiating is having your fiancé(e) or significant other included in the relocation package. Again, you should explain the situation and *ask* if it would be possible to have this person included. Whatever their answer is, it should be regarded as final. If the company policy prohibits including significant others in relocation, they're certainly not going to make an exception for an entry level offer.

The bottom line is that offers for entry level jobs are basically nonnegotiable. Even if you're lucky enough to be deciding between two or more offers, you won't gain anything by trying to negotiate and leverage one offer against another. With the possible exceptions I indicated, you should view an offer the way the company does: Take it or leave it.

Most offers will include a decision date by which you must respond or consider the offer withdrawn. When you think about it, this is nonnegotiable as well. You've told this company that you really want to work for them. You've asked them for the job several times. How do you think you look if you ask them for more time? If the offer fails to include a decision date you should ask for clarification. Whatever date they give you should be considered final.

Accepting Offers: Let's assume for a minute that you're offered a job that meets both all of your essential criteria and all of your desired criteria. You're certain that the offer is exactly what you want. Let's also assume that the offer is made verbally. Here's what I would recommend that you say:

"Thank you very much. I'm very excited about the opportunity and look forward to starting on the date that you stated. Would you please send me an offer letter and a benefits package? Once I get the offer letter, I'll sign it and return it so that you will have my formal acceptance. I'm looking forward to working for you."

This reinforces your professionalism. It also gives you a few days to think about the offer and resolve any questions that may surface. Should you also have an opportunity pending that is even more appealing to you, you should call that company's recruiting officer immediately. Tell him or her that you have a good offer but would really prefer his or her company. Give that person your time constraints. If that company can make you an offer in time, you will accept it. Otherwise, you'll accept the first offer. It's a nice situation in that you win either way.

The importance of the offer letter is that once you sign it and mail it back to them, you have a *contract* that obligates them to hire you on the stated terms. If the next month brings a hiring freeze to that company, they will still have to honor their offer. The real beauty of the offer letter is that they're making all of the commitments. If you change your mind for whatever reason, you won't have to go to work for them. While legally they could sue you for specific performance (to start the job as contracted or to be held in contempt of court), pragmatically no company wants a new employee who isn't happy to be there. However, unless you have a very good explanation for not honoring your commitment, you clearly will have burned a bridge.

Now that I've raised the issue, I'd like to give you some perspective on a question that I'm often asked. "Is it okay to accept an offer and keep looking?" My answer is probably not, unless there are unusual circumstances. As far as the moral and ethical issues involved, I leave that to you, your value system, and the circumstances. Personally, I believe that a person's word is sacred, and that once you have accepted an offer you should terminate your search. Pragmatically, you should be aware that most industries are like fraternities where everybody knows everybody. The person you accepted a job from and subsequently rejected might become your boss next year.

Rejecting Offers: When you receive multiple offers, you will be in the position of having to reject all but the best one. Even though you turn down a company's offer, you should look to reinforce their excellent judgment in making you the offer. Even if you reject the offer verbally, you should follow it with a short letter. In the letter you should thank them for the flattering offer and the opportunity that they extended to you. Never indicate any negatives about the company that impacted your difficult decision. List several positive aspects that appealed to you. Close with a parting thought that you hope your paths will cross again in order to leave open the possibility of working together in the future. In two years you may find that that company now offers you exactly what you're looking for, or that a key member of the interview team has moved to another company that you now want to work for, or even moves to your company and becomes your boss!

On a few occasions I have recruited candidates for an opening who expressed the following concern when I told them which company I was recruiting for: "I'm very interested. But I rejected an offer from that company when I graduated." In most cases, the company's response has been to check their records to see how the candidate handled the situation. I never have had a company refuse to interview such a candidate as long as that candidate had rejected the previous offer in a professional manner. The bottom line is that you never know where the future will lead you. Be smart and keep your options open.

Deciding Among Offers: It will never cease to amaze me that when job seekers receive more than one offer, they often struggle and agonize over the decision as if they have a colossal problem. The reality is that it's really an easy decision to make, if you look at it objectively instead of emotionally. Let me share a technique that I regularly use with candidates who are trying to decide if they should stay where they are or accept an offer to move to another company.

Take out a sheet of paper. Down the lefthand column write down your essential criteria, followed by your desired criteria. Now, for each job, make columns to the right. List all the attributes of each job as they relate to your criteria. Below your attributes for each job, list any additional positives. Below the positives for each job, list any negatives that you can think of. Eliminate any offers that fail to satisfy your essential criteria. (If none of the offers satisfies your essential criteria completely, don't eliminate any offers yet.) For each offer, cross out what you consider to be comparable attributes. For example, if your desired criteria include living in either New York City or Chicago, and you have an offer from each city, eliminate that attribute (location). Do the same for your list of additional positives and negatives. When you consider compensation, don't make the mistake of comparing absolute salary dollars. Utilize a cost-of-living index for each location to determine the standard of living that that salary will give you. (You'll have a higher standard of living on $25,000 per year in Winston-Salem than you will on $30,000 per year in New York City.) It's not important that attributes, positives, and negatives be categorically the same to be eliminated. What is essential is that they rank as equally important to you. Once you complete your objective analysis, you'll be left with a few attributes, positives, and negatives that didn't cancel each other out. *These represent the real differences between the offers.* Generally, the objective answer will now be self-evident. If you prefer to sleep on it overnight, fine. But keep in mind that you're about to start your career. A key element of almost any successful career is the ability to make decisions quickly and to live with them. It should be comforting to maintain the perspective that you're only making a decision about your first job.

Celebrate: Congratulations on your new job. You've put a lot of effort and time into finding the job that's right for you. You've learned several valuable skills on how to look for a job, skills that you will have for the rest of your life.

Make a point of celebrating your success. You have certainly earned it. Bask in the glory of what you have achieved. There's a whole new world and life that you'll be embarking on soon. Don't ever make the mistake of forgetting to enjoy every phase of your journey.

Chapter Seven

Jump-Starting Your Career

Building the Right Foundation for a Successful Career

Soon you'll be taking the first step down your career path. It's a journey that will probably last for many decades and lead you to many interesting and, hopefully, rewarding places. As we've seen with finding your first job, great careers don't just happen; they take planning and hard work. However, as with landing your first job, you'll find that there's tremendous satisfaction to be gained from your accomplishments. What I'm going to do in this final chapter is to give you the benefit of over fifteen years of experience in corporate America, so that you can jump-start your career.

The most startling revelation to me was that doing a good job is only one factor in being successful. I've watched people with only marginal talent and limited accomplishments rise up the corporate ladder to become president. I've watched exceptionally talented people languish in middle management. Luck and timing clearly play a significant role; however, I'm going to give you a few strategies that will put a lucky rabbit's foot in your career's hip pocket.

Plan a Vacation: If your finances and your start date permit it, you should take a long vacation before you begin your first job. Spend the summer in Europe, take an extended camping trip in Canada, or do whatever turns you on. It's likely to be a long time before you're in a position again to take a one- or two-month vacation. You've been used to lots of vacation time while you were a student. Even if you worked every summer, you probably had a change of scenery, and you certainly had a change of pace. In all probability, it will be several years before you are allowed to take more than two weeks of vacation each year.

Not only will you show up at work well rested and ready to start learning and contributing, but you'll have some recent interesting experiences to help you to build your initial interpersonal relationships. Even if you need to borrow a little money for your adventure, I would encourage you to do so. After all, your income is about to increase dramatically, compared to school. If necessary, go to a bank and have your parents cosign and guarantee the loan. (It will also establish a good credit rating for you when you go to finance a car or your first home.)

Save Your Records: By the time you've successfully completed your job search, you will have probably generated a significant amount of information about the companies and the people in the industry you are now a part of. Some of this information could prove to be valuable in your current job. If you ran a multifunctional or multi-industry search, you may decide in a year or two that you chose the wrong (for you) industry and be in the position of looking for a job in the other industry that you've already researched. It's also possible that in a couple of years you'll love the industry you're in but want to change companies. If you save your records, you'll save some time.

Probably the best reason to save your records is to be in a position to easily help someone conducting a job search in the same area(s) that you did. Whether it's your best friend, or a friend of a friend, the more favors you are able to do for people, the more due bills you will have to ask people for favors to help your career progress. It's a great asset to have in your career building block foundation. Whenever you're in a position to easily do someone a favor, you should. Don't make the mistake of prejudging the value of the due bill. You may be very surprised in a couple of years to learn who the new young superstars are.

Set Goals: Remember when you were planning your job-hunting campaign, I told you that the first rule of sales is to plan your work and work your plan. The same principle applies to launching and maintaining a successful career. Before you start your job, you should sit down and commit to writing your career goals for at least the first five years. Your goals should include the target dates for your first two promotions. If you have enough direction, it's even better to establish your goals even further out.

Try to be realistic, but if you see yourself as a fast tracker, there's nothing wrong with having aggressive goals. Down the road, it's one of the ways to objectively measure if your career track is on target, where you are, or if you need to change companies to get your career back on the course you established. You should regularly review your goals, and plan to either change or reestablish them annually. They're your goals, so you should focus on whatever is important to you, whether it's money, title, responsibility, or any meaningful combination.

Just because you fail to achieve one of your goals doesn't mean that you won't achieve the next one. Maybe your first promotion goal was unrealistic, or you're a late bloomer. As you gain more real-world experience, you'll be able to establish more realistic goals in your annual revision.

The other key element in achieving your goals is to develop the strategies that you'll need. Understand what you need to accomplish on the job so that you can focus your efforts where they'll benefit you the most.

Your First Month Working: There are two similarities between your first few weeks at a new job and your first few weeks at the school from which you just graduated. You have a great deal of learning to do, and everybody comes in fresh with no background baggage. Nobody knows your past, which means that you are in a position to change anything about yourself. Obviously, you're not going to become an entirely new person, but there may be one or two things about yourself that you want to change. Perhaps you've always had a reputation as the class clown. A good sense of humor is always an asset, but being viewed as the court jester will never get you a seat on the throne. Maybe your language has become too frequently peppered with crass four-letter words. Think about it *before* your first day on the job. You'll never be in a better position to make a change or two.

When I told you about interviewing strategy, I stressed the importance of first impressions. Not surprisingly, first impressions are also important when you start working. I don't mean to imply that your first day on the job will make or break your career, but the first month on the job in any company is usually important, especially if you have fast-track ambitions. Right or wrong, after a new employee has been on the job a month or so, most corporate managers make a preliminary evaluation and place them in one of three categories. The choices are 1) probable fast tracker, 2) probable solid performer, or 3) possible bad hire. Obviously, you want to avoid the third category. The point is that human nature results in it being more difficult to change someone's mind once they've made a decision. If they do change their mind and reclassify you, it's more likely that they'll move you down, not up, in their estimation.

I told you earlier that your first job starts out as the most intense learning experience you will ever have. Fortunately, you're exceptionally well prepared. The most important skill that you acquired in school was learning how to learn. Now you're going to take full advantage of that education. Don't make the mistake of coming in with the attitude that you're going to impress them immediately by teaching them a better way to do something. Although you may be able to, your lack of experience can also manifest in your better way making you look foolish, because you lack the experience and perspective that can only be acquired over time. As I said, you've still got a *lot* to learn.

My counsel is to fill your first month at work consuming "ALEs." ALEs is my shorthand for *A*sking questions, *L*istening carefully to the answers, and *E*ducating yourself. Of course you will have to perform whatever tasks they assign to you, but get in the habit of asking questions until you understand not only what you're doing, but how it fits into the big picture as well. If you think that your company is doing something badly and you think you know a better way, you should adopt the Socratic approach of ALEs. Ask why something is or is not being handled the way it is. If upon hearing the explanation, you still think that your way is better, don't recommend, ask why it wouldn't make sense to do it your way. If your way is really better, you have a much better chance of having your idea adopted and implemented. You'll still get the credit for the contribution when you are right. But if your idea has no merit, you'll learn why as you continue your on-the-job education. In addition, you won't have recommended something that isn't right; you merely asked questions about what you're doing. Trust me, a steady diet of ALEs is the ideal way both to create the image that you want and to learn what you need to know to be successful. Even after you have extensive experience, ALEs is a very effective way of dealing with people at work, making recommendations, and even managing people.

My final counsel to you is to develop the habit of recording and quantifying your accomplishments. There's never as good a time to quantify the impact of an accomplishment as when you achieve it, and the results are fresh in your mind and readily available. There are two important reasons for documenting and quantifying your contributions. First of all, you'll want to know what you've accomplished so that you can decide if your contributions are fully appreciated when you are given your performance reviews. Second, if the future finds you either wanting, or needing, to find a new job, it will be easy to update your résumé with your quantified accomplishments.

This is where we part company. You've learned many important new skills to get your first job and to get your career off to a fast start. Maybe as you progress up the corporate ladder, you'll be calling me to handle a strategic consulting assignment for you. Whether or not our paths ever cross again, you have my sincerest best wishes for a successful, rewarding career and a happy life. Whatever your goals are, I hope that you realize them.

Appendix

ACCOUNTING: *Accounting Firms Directory,* American Business Directories, Inc., Published Annually

ADVERTISING: *Standard Directory of Advertising Agencies,* National Register Publishing Company, Inc., Published Annually and *Advertising Career Directory,* Career Press Inc., Editor: Ronald W. Fry, 1992

AEROSPACE/DEFENSE: *Aerospace Companies,* DMSINC, Published Annually and *World Aviation Directory,* Murdoch Magazines, Published Annually.

APPAREL/TEXTILES: *Fairchild's Textile and Apparel Financial Directory,* Fairchild Books, Published Annually and *Davidson's Textile Blue Book,* Davidson Publishing Company, Published Annually

AUTOMOTIVE: *Ward's Automotive Yearbook,* Ward's Communications, Inc., Published Annually

BANKING/FINANCE: *Moody's Bank and Finance Manual,* Moody's Investors Service, Published Annually and *Securities*

Industry Yearbook, Securities Industry Association, Editor: Rosaile Pepe, Published Annually

BIOTECH: *The Biotechnology Directory,* Stockton Press, Published Annually

COMMUNICATIONS: *Telecommunications Directory,* Gale Research, Inc., Editor: John Krol, 1991

DIRECT MAIL: *Mail Order Business Directory,* B. Klein Publications, Inc., Published Annually

EDUCATION: *Directory of Public School Systems in the U.S.,* Assoc. for school, college, and university staffing, Editor: Charles A. Marshall, Published Annually

ELECTRONICS: *Electronic News Financial Fact Book and Directory,* Fairchild Publications, Inc., Published Annually

ENERGY: *Moody's Public Utility Manual,* Moody's Investor Services, Inc., Published Annually, and *Whole World Oil Directory,* National Register Publishing Company, Published Annually

FOOD: *Thomas Grocery Registry,* Thomas Publishing Company, Published Annually

GENERAL: *Directories in Print,* Gale Research Inc., Editor: Charles Montney, 1992, Published in even years

GOVERNMENT/PUBLIC SERVICE: *Complete Guide to Public Employment,* Impact Publications, Ron & Cary Krannich, 1992

HEALTH CARE: *Dunn's Guide to Health Care Companies,* Dunn & Bradstreet, Published Annually, and *Billian's Hospital Bluebook,* Billian Publishing, Editor: Sandra McBrayer, Published Annually

HOTELS/RESORTS: *Official Hotel and Resort Guide,* and *Travel Weekly's World Travel Directory,* both Published Annually by Murdoch Magazines

INFORMATION PROCESSING: *Business Software Directory,* Information Sources, Inc., Editor: Ruth K. Koolish, Published Annually, and *Telecommunications Directory,* Gale Research, Inc., Editor: John Krol, Published every odd year

INTERNSHIPS: *Internships* (Four Volumes Covering: Accounting, Advertising, Banking, Brokerage, Finance, Insurance, Marketing, Sales, Public Relations, etc.), Published by Career Press

Inc. (1-800-Career1 or 201-427-0229), Editor: Ronald W. Fry at $11.95 per volume

INSURANCE: *Insurance Almanac,* Underwriter Printing and Publishing Company, Editor: Donald E. Wolff, Published Annually

JOURNALISM: *Bacon's Media Alerts,* Bacon's Publishing Company, Inc. Editor: Wilfrid W. Budd, Published Annually

MINING: *International Directory of Mining,* McGraw-Hill Publishing Company, Published Annually

MOTION PICTURES/BROADCASTING: *Bacon's Radio/TV Directory,* Bacon's Publishing Company Inc., Editor: Wilfrid W. Budd, Published Annually and *International Motion Picture Almanac,* Quigley Publishing Company, Inc., Published Annually

MUSIC/VIDEO: *International Buyer's Guide,* Billboard Publications, Published Annually

NON-PROFIT: *The Foundation Directory,* The Foundation Center, Published every odd year with even year supplements

PHARMACEUTICAL INDUSTRY: *Pharmaceutical Marketers Directory,* Fisher-Stevens Publications, Published Annually

PUBLISHING: *Literary Market Place: The Directory of American Book Publishing,* R. R. Bowker Company, Published Annually and *Working Press of the Nation* (5 Volumes), National Research Bureau, Inc., Editor: Nancy O. Veatch, Published Annually

REAL ESTATE: *Directory of Real Estate Investors & Commercial Real Estate Brokers,* National Register Publishing Company, Inc., Published Annually

RESEARCH & DEVELOPMENT: *Research Centers Directory,* Gale Research Company, Published Annually

RETAILING: *Fairchild's Financial Manual of Retail Stores,* Fairchild Books, Published Annually, and see *Directories in Print* under "General" section for directories specific to different types of retail outlets

TRANSPORTATION: *Moody's Transportation Manual,* Dunn & Bradstreet Company, Published Annually

Index